Praise for Debra Haffner's books

WHAT EVERY 21ST-CENTURY PARENT NEEDS TO KNOW
Facing Today's Challenges with Wisdom and Heart

"From child development research, public health, faith traditions, and sexuality education, Debra Haffner has amassed a deep lake of knowledge....This book empowers parents [with] buckets of practical advice." —Karen Hein, M.D., former President,
William T. Grant Foundation

"Debra Haffner's latest book will appeal to all parents, whether conservative or liberal. Her no-nonsense advice will help parents give *their* values to their children." —Rev. Bob Edgar,
President of Common Cause,
former General Secretary of the National Council of Churches

"Parents could not ask for a better guide than this warm, wise, resourceful book that will help any family understand what works best for keeping their children safe and strong." —Nell Minow,
"The Movie Mom," Beliefnet.com

"Although raising children seems daunting at best and sometimes impossible, Debra Haffner encourages modern parents to feel they are up to the task. In fact, reading *What Every 21st-Century Parent Needs to Know* made me feel better about the choices I've made as a mom. I actually feel less afraid of all the bad influences that bombard our kids since reading it." —Lisa Birnbach, Radio Show Host,
Author of *1,003 Great Things About Kids*
and *The Official Preppy Handbook*

From Diapers to Dating
A Parent's Guide to Raising Sexually Healthy Children

"A valuable book...to develop a comfortable, ongoing constructive rapport with your children about sex." —*Washington Post*

"An excellent guide...Haffner's message is practical and frank, both forward-looking and nonpermissive....Essential." —*Library Journal*

"Accessible and forthright, this book is full of advice to help parents teach their children to feel good about themselves and their sexuality." —*Richmond Parents Monthly* (Richmond, VA)

"Realistic, practical, and informative—the best kind of guide for being a better parent....Haffner [offers] a clear-eyed assist with deciding what sexual values to impart to children, and then advice on coupling those values with accurate, age-appropriate information." —*Kirkus Reviews*

Beyond the Big Talk
A Parent's Guide to Raising Sexually Healthy Teens

"Picking up from where her first book left off, Haffner explores the choppy seas of adolescence, from middle school to college...and offers solid advice and resources to parents, who will greatly appreciate her candor." —*Booklist*

"Writing in an engaging style, Haffner addresses the individual topics families face at different points in adolescence. This highly recommended resource is sure to be welcomed by parents of teenagers—and future teenagers—everywhere." —Voices of Youth Advocates

"Credible and reassuring, Haffner carefully articulates what the range of values might be on a particular issue, but makes it clear that it is up to parents to convey their own values to their children." —*Family Life Matters*, Rutgers University

WHAT EVERY
21st-CENTURY PARENT
NEEDS TO KNOW

*Facing Today's Challenges
with Wisdom and Heart*

DEBRA W. HAFFNER

 *Newmarket Press   New York*

This book is designed to provide accurate and authoritative information based on the best parenting practices at the time of this writing. It is not intended as a substitute for medical or mental health advice.

Copyright © 2008 by Debra W. Haffner

All rights reserved. This book may not be reproduced, in whole or in part, in any form, without written permission. Inquiries should be addressed to Permissions Department, Newmarket Press, 18 East 48th Street, New York, NY 10017.

This book is published in the United States of America.

First Edition

ISBN: 978-1-55704-726-7 (paper) ISBN: 978-1-55704-787-8 (hardcover)

10 9 8 7 6 5 4 3 2 1   10 9 8 7 6 5 4 3 2 1

Library of Congress Cataloging-in-Publication Data
Haffner, Debra.
  What every 21st-century parent needs to know: facing today's
challenges with wisdom and heart / Debra W. Haffner.—1st ed.
      p. cm.
  Includes bibliographical references and index.
  ISBN 978-1-55704-787-8 (hardcover: alk. paper)—ISBN 978-1-55704-
726-7 (pbk.: alk. paper) 1. Parenting—United States. I. Title.
HQ755.8.H3314 2008
649'.10973—dc22   2007036508

QUANTITY PURCHASES

Companies, professional groups, clubs, and other organizations may qualify for special terms when ordering quantities of this title. For information or a catalog, write Special Sales Department, Newmarket Press, 18 East 48th Street, New York, NY 10017; call (212) 832-3575; fax (212) 832-3629; or e-mail info@newmarketpress.com.

www.newmarketpress.com

Designed by M. J. Di Massi

Manufactured in the United States of America.

To Cynthia Baber, Rosella Fanelli, Barbara Fast, Ledell Mulvaney, Barbara Levi-Berliner, Tess O'Brien, and Jodi Wallace, who journey with me in parenting and life.

Contents

Acknowledgments

WRITING A BOOK is a solitary act. Life is not. I am blessed in life by a loving family, a strong network of friends, and brilliant and insightful colleagues. I have felt their presence behind me, supporting me, as I worked on this book.

Many people generously provided information, resources, interviews, and ideas. In alphabetical order, I am indebted to Dr. Andrea G. Barthwell, Dr. Jonathan Fast, Marc Fernandes, Dr. Bill Finger, Dr. Susan Finkelstein, Dr. Merle Hamburger, Dr. David Hanson, Dr. Sandra Hofferth, Dr. Michael Males, and Dr. Bob Selverstone, who freely gave of their time and expertise for in-depth interviews. I am especially grateful to Barbara Levi-Berliner for her gracious sharing of ideas based on her thirty years as a social worker specializing in parenting issues.

Two people deserve special mention in this list: Dr. Kate Ott and Alison Boyle. Both helped me locate research, articles, PDF files, and authors, and prepare reference lists. Alison, a recent graduate of Boston College, provided the first draft of the Appendix, Resources for More Information. My niece, Emily Wallace, a junior at Manhattanville College, checked the final references and resources.

Several colleagues volunteered to read this book when it was in draft and offer comments based on their particular expertise. I am so appreciative of reviews by Kathleen Baldwin, Consuelo Bonillas,

Rev. Steve Clapp, Dr. Merle Hamburger, Lis Maurer, Susan Milstein, and Danene Sorace. This book is better for their insights; the mistakes, of course, are all mine.

Writing a book in the midst of raising children and my full-time ministry with the Religious Institute on Sexual Morality, Justice, and Healing was sometimes stressful, to say the least. My most productive writing was done on retreat, away from the requirements of daily life. I am grateful to my husband, Ralph Tartaglione, for filling in for my absences, but also to the people who generously shared their homes for me to write in: my sister-in-law Pat Grande; my friends in Boston and Maine, Ellen Remmer and Chris Fox; Kathryn Booth and Joan Grant in Seal Cove in Acadia, Maine; Jane Fonda in New Mexico; and Esther Margolis and Stan Fisher in Amagansett.

Esther Margolis, the President of Newmarket Press, has become more than my publisher; she is my friend. She not only trusted me with her weekend house to write in, she has been a cheerleader for this book and for my previous two parenting books from the beginning. Many of my friends who are authors complain about their publishers; I have always felt supported and nurtured by Esther and the rest of the Newmarket staff, and I am deeply grateful.

Susan Hans O'Connor shepherded this book through the editing process. She was a gracious, kind, and supportive editor, and she was helpful beyond words in shaping the final version of this book. It was truly a pleasure to work with her.

I rely heavily in this book on research on children and adolescents' well-being. I am so appreciative of the foresight, dedication, and scholarship of the many people from the U.S. Centers for Disease Control who have compiled the Youth Risk Behavior Study for the past fifteen years, the University of Michigan staff who have done the Monitoring the Future study for the past thirty, the Search Institute for their work on developmental assets and spirituality, and the Guttmacher Institute for their work on everything about sexuality and reproductive health. Untold numbers of researchers, assistants, data analyzers, and secretaries have worked for decades now to help understand children and young people's behaviors; they are indeed unsung heroes. I also am indebted to the creators of Google

Scholar; my first books required untold trips to libraries, but Google Scholar allowed me access to the finest research journals wherever I was.

I am very grateful to all the parents who shared their personal stories, problems, and ideas with me. They have included my friends, the congregants at the Unitarian Church in Westport, and colleagues across the country. They also include the strangers whose lives I often unwittingly observed and recount in this book. To protect their and their children's confidentiality, I will not name them here, and I have changed the details of their stories to make them unrecognizable to those who know them.

Even more important to this book are the people in my life who have helped me become a better parent. It indeed takes a village to raise a child. Younger women often ask me how I have been able to raise two children and have a successful career as an advocate, author, and now minister. I always answer, "I married the right man." Ralph Tartaglione has been my partner for nearly thirty years now and my spouse for twenty-five; my appreciation goes beyond words.

I dedicate this book to the women in my women's group, past and present, who have been meeting monthly since 1991; we have shared each step of parenting, the highs and the lows, and I cannot imagine my life without them in it. I know that they will not agree with me on everything I have written here, but I also know that they will celebrate its publication with me.

And finally, although in reality first, I thank my children, Alyssa Haffner Tartaglione and Gregory Joseph Haffner Tartaglione, for teaching me how to be a better parent. They graciously allow me in this volume, as well as my previous books, to share stories from their own lives, although each retained veto power over what I was able to share. They both have said that they have sometimes felt like the test cases of my theories, and argue about whether it was worse to be the daughter of a sex educator or a "preacher's kid." I know that having a mother with both of my careers has its challenges. They are my finest teachers and the heart of my life.

INTRODUCTION

Is Parenting Harder Today?

TWO HUNDRED PEOPLE fill the middle school auditorium. They are parents of children ranging in age from two to seventeen. As I have done for the past seven years traveling across the country, talking to parent groups, I begin by asking, "Is it harder to be a parent today than when we were children?" Almost everyone raises a hand. Then I ask them why they think so.

People call out answers. "Drugs. Alcohol. Out-of-control kids. Hooking up. AIDS. School violence. The Internet. MySpace. The media. Pressure to succeed. Thongs." Most of them laugh or nod their heads in agreement. And public opinion polls demonstrate that these moms and dads are far from alone. Almost 8 in 10 parents think it is much harder to be a parent today than when they were children. But is it really?

There is no doubt that parents today feel overwhelmed by the rapidly changing world that their children seem so easily to embrace. Parents often seem to be seeking an elusive sense of balance. They rush home from work to rush their children to soccer practice, to piano lessons, stopping for fast food before their children come home to begin homework and then IM all their friends. Parents fall into bed exhausted and then start all over again the next day. Not surprisingly, their children are often as stressed out as they are. I sometimes feel this way myself.

Of course, parenting today is challenging, but the truth is that it has always been challenging. The late 1960s, 70s, and early 80s were especially difficult times in which to parent—when we were the ones being parented! The challenges simply change with the times.

"BEWARE THE WALTZ!"

Parents and other adults have always worried about the next generation of young people; it almost seems that we are hardwired to forget our own youthful excesses. Every generation of adults has had a hard time adapting to new social changes that come easily to our children. Many of us now are worried about our children misusing the Internet and cell phones; our grandparents were worried about how our parents would misuse TV. And our parents were very worried about us when we were adolescents. Media stories abounded in the 70s and early 80s about how out of control we were. Look at these *Time* magazine cover stories from our generation:

1969 "Drugs and the Young"

1972 "Teenage Sex: Letting the Pendulum Swing"

1985 "Children Having Children"

Those of us who are part of the late baby boom (born between 1956 and 1964) or the beginning of Generation X (born between 1965 and 1970) did not receive the media or public attention of the earlier boomers (born between 1946 and 1955), but were actually more likely to have been involved in teenage risk-taking behaviors. Social observers wrote that the children of the 1950s and 1960s were "overvalued children" because of postwar mobility and increasing suburbanization, which led parents to turn more to Dr. Spock than to their own parents for advice. More than one commentator bemoaned that we should have been spanked, not Spocked. Unlike our older brothers and sisters, we were less political but more likely to use drugs and to have casual sex.

Many women who parented the late boomers, now in their seventies and eighties, have admitted to me that they were almost frightened of us as teenagers. Among other things, they worried about our clothes, the boys' long hair, our rebellion against the Vietnam War, acid rock, the possibility that we were experimenting with LSD and other drugs, and increasing sexual freedom. Indeed, the percentage of teenagers in high school having sexual intercourse increased two-thirds between 1971 and 1979.

As I will discuss more in the sexuality chapter, it was teenagers in the 1970s who set the norms for today's sexual and dating behavior. During the later baby-boom and Gen X years of adolescence, the number of young people using illegal drugs and having sexual intercourse in high school began increasing to today's levels. Perhaps it was because our parents, who came of age in the 1940s and 50s, had such trouble understanding and coping with the massive changes of civil rights, women's, and gay and lesbian movements of the 1960s and 70s and thus resisted setting limits for their children that many of us do not feel confident about our parenting today.

But we weren't the first generation to challenge adults—far from it. The very nature of parenting is anxiety-producing, and adults have always worried that the current generation of young people was going to upend the world. It may surprise you to know that what Tom Brokaw called the "Greatest Generation" of young men (today's grandfathers and great-grandfathers) were described by the Surgeon General of the Army at the time as lacking "the ability to face life, live with others, think for themselves, and stand on their own two feet." In 1951, *Time* magazine noted in an alarming report that "authorities have become aware of a tremendous and frightening spread of narcotic addiction among teens." A 1956 article worried that "teenagers laugh at parents' fears that rock and roll is a menace to morals." That was my mother's generation.

Actually, as long ago as 1816, the *Times* of London warned parents about the "indecent foreign dance called the Waltz." They described it this way: "It is quite sufficient to cast one's eyes on the voluptuous intertwining of the limbs and close compressure of the bodies to see that it is far indeed removed from the modest reserve which has hitherto been considered distinctive of English females." They concluded in an ominous tone: "We feel a duty to warn every parent against exposing his daughter to so fatal a contagion." Remember that the next time you receive a note home from the middle school principal about banning too-close dancing at the school dance.

Concerns about managing children were often raised by religious leaders through the centuries. Some religious points of view saw children as inherently sinful creatures and born into original sin. The Protestant reformer John Calvin wrote that "the whole nature [of children] is a seed of sin; thus it cannot be but hateful and abominable to God." Jonathan Edwards, the colonial preacher, wrote of unbaptized infants that they are but "young vipers, and infinitely more hateful than vipers." The Book of Deuteronomy (21: 18–21) taught that a "wayward and defiant son who does not heed his father and mother and does not obey them even after they discipline him" should be brought to a "public place of his community" so that "the men of his town shall stone him to death." (Alternate views exist about the innocence and goodness of children in Scripture as well; children are a blessing from God throughout much of the Bible, and Jesus asks his followers to become like children to enter the dominion of heaven.) Socrates, hundreds of years before the Common Era, is said by Plato to have complained thusly about youth:

> The children now love luxury; they have bad manners, contempt for authority; they allow disrespect for elders and love chatter in place of exercise. Children now are tyrants, not the servants of their households. They no longer rise when elders enter the room. They contradict their parents, chatter before company, gobble up dainties at the table, cross their legs, and tyrannize their teachers.

Sound familiar?

Parents of all generations seem to experience anxiety about their children, but one of the biggest differences today is the almost daily reports in the media to scare us. As I was writing this chapter, a headline on the cover of the latest issue of *Reader's Digest* screamed out to me in the grocery store checkout line: "The New Great Threat to Your Children." I felt a little less threatened when I looked closer and saw that it was an article about sports injuries. Full-page ads from the Partnership for a Drug-Free America warn us that marijuana is much more dangerous today than it was thirty years ago—but is it? It seems that every other child is taking a medication for a learning disorder. Are there more children with learning disabilities who need to be medicated today? Is it true that the additives in meat and milk are causing our children to reach puberty earlier? Is there an oral sex epidemic among thirteen-year-olds? Is the risk of my child being kidnapped or sexually abused higher than when we were children?

The media fuel our fears—and our confusion. What is a parent to believe; what is a parent to do? Is there any good news to share? In chapter 1, I'll introduce the realities of parenting in the twenty-first century, and explore these in greater depth in chapters 2 to 9.

"STATISTICS DON'T LIE"—OR DO THEY?

The scary media stories we hear are often centered on some alarming-sounding statistics. Should we believe everything we hear or read? When I was getting my master's degree in public health, during my very first class in biostatistics, the professor shared with us this axiom: "Statistics do not lie. People lie with statistics."

How facts are presented makes a big difference in how we will react to them. For example, one can accurately say that obesity rates have tripled among children and adolescents during the past two decades. Alternately, one can accurately say that the percentage of children who are obese has grown from 5 percent in the early 1980s to 17 percent today. Or, even more reassuringly, 83 percent of American children are at a healthy weight, twice as many as adults. All are correct, but only one is a media headline that raises parents' alarm and sells newspapers. As I'll talk about in depth in chapter 3, we do need to be concerned about children's physical health and nutrition, but most of us don't need to view our children and teens as being "in crisis" on that score. You will see many examples throughout this book of this kind of "distortion" that can often create misplaced anxiety in parents.

WHAT IS HELPFUL TO PARENTS?

The shelves at the bookstore are filled with tomes on binge drinking, bullying, eating disorders, and out-of-control teenagers, books with titles like *Stressed-Out Girls, Binge, Mean Girls, Parenting Your Out-of-Control Teenager*, and even *Daddy Needs a Drink*. There are plenty of books to play into your insecurity about your ability to be a good parent, and then offer you ten easy steps to quell that anxiety.

This is not one of those books. This book is about how to deal most effectively with the real (as opposed to the media-created) challenges we face as parents in the twenty-first century. It also shares the good news about parenting today, which we don't hear often enough. There is a lot of good news about children and teenagers, there is a lot that we as parents are doing very well, but there is also the good news that we can learn to be even more effective parents. I will show you that by using a style I call Affirming Parenthood, we can increase our chances of having healthy and happy children.

In other words, I will describe how the way we parent our children can make a difference. I will help you look at how many of the media reports about tweens and teens today are making us unnecessarily anxious, and how these fears may actually be hurting our children. I will occasionally remind you of how difficult we were as teenagers. I will address what is different about parenting in the twenty-first century and what has not changed. I think you will be both surprised and reassured.

For example, did you know that child kidnappings, sexual abuse of children, and the teenage birth rate are all down? That the vast majority of children, tweens, and teens like and feel close to their parents? But I know how hard it is not to feel anxious about our children. While I was finishing this book, my daughter, Alyssa, was completing her senior year of college and my son, Gregory, was finishing the eighth grade. Like you, I love being a parent, and nothing has given me as much satisfaction in my life. I am deeply grateful for my children. Every morning when I wake, I feel blessed that they are happy and healthy. I'm sure most of you feel the same—you wouldn't trade parenthood for anything. I am also a minister and a sexuality educator, and I work with hundreds of parents each year who share their concerns and anxieties about their children with me. What I have learned is that parents often feel stressed-out, alone, and in need of help. I hope this book will provide you some help, hope, and comfort.

I am going to assume that if you are reading this book you are probably already committed to being the best parent you can be. You have questions, you have parenting problems, you are confused about what you hear about children and teenagers in the media and from your friends, but you are committed to raising your children well.

So I am not going to spend time talking about what parents should not do. I am taking it as a given that you do not physically or sexually abuse your children, expose them to sexual abuse or sexually explicit information, or physically or emotionally abuse your partner or any of the children in your household. You know that if you abuse alcohol or other substances, struggle with an acute untreated mental illness, or engage in criminal behavior, your ability to parent well is severely compromised. If you do face such problems, you need to deal with these crushing issues first. Get help, and make sure your children are receiving adequate support from other caring adults while you do.

No book is going to be much help to you or your children if they are already in big trouble. If you are concerned that your child is using drugs, is failing school, has an eating disorder, is sexually involved before the age of fourteen, or suffers from a mental illness, please make an appointment today with a qualified professional.

The Appendix at the end of the book lists organizations that can help you find the professional support you need.

You do not have to be a parent to gain insights from this book. Many people play an important role in children's and teenagers' lives. Research tells us that it is important for young people to have significant adults in their lives besides their parents. So I hope that whether you are a teacher, coach, minister, rabbi, imam, aunt, uncle, or grandparent, you will find this book helpful as well.

NO GUARANTEES

This book does not pretend to come with a money-back guarantee. "Good parenting" does not come with a warranty for "good kids." I wish it did. According to a 1998 report by the U.S. Centers for Disease Control and Prevention, in addition to parents, "peers, media, social norms, developmental needs, access to substances...genetic predispositions, cognitive factors, emotional considerations (e.g., self-esteem, future orientation, risk perceptions) and academic achievement...influence a young person's health and well being." So does the fit between a parent's and child's temperament, family history, family functioning, birth order, sibling influence, and the child's schools, community agencies, and faith-based institutions. In other words, you are vitally important, but it is not all about you!

The research I will share in this book offers perspectives on which parenting behaviors generally have a positive influence on young people, but there is no such thing as a strategy or technique that works on every child, and what worked one year may not work the next. For example, as we will see in the chapter on sex, alcohol, and drugs, a teen anticipating serious negative consequences from using alcohol is much less likely to drink, but the risk does not go down to zero. Teens who participate in religious education have half the rate of sexual intercourse as teens in the general population, but a third of them are still having intercourse. In other words, certain parenting strategies have a positive influence, but nothing a parent does will reduce a child's involvement in risk-taking behaviors to zero.

To keep things in perspective, you should realize that at least half of teenagers will engage in some behavior that we as adults would prefer them not to, at least once or twice, but taking a risk now and then does not mean that your child is in trouble. And by their early twenties, many young people will have "aged out" of such misbehavior. (As I was taught on the first day of public health school, the risk to an individual regardless of population studies is always 1 or 0.)

You can do everything as well as you can (at least most of the time) and your children may still try tobacco, alcohol, and other drugs, still become sexually involved before they (or you!) are ready, still cut classes or have trouble with school, and still suffer from depression or other mental illnesses. No wonder we are anxious.

The good news is that even in the most challenging circumstances, good parenting seems to make a difference. The choices we make and the parenting practices we use can greatly increase our chances of raising a child who becomes a happy, productive adult. Good parents know that they make a difference in their children's lives and seek to be the best possible parents. The family counselors I know generally agree that it is rare to see a child or teenager facing serious social problems without finding out that the family as a whole is facing serious dysfunctions. It happens, usually when the child or teen has a biochemically based mental health problem, but it is uncommon.

I am not going to try to make you anxious about your parenting skills and then tell you that if you follow my instructions, everything will turn out okay. I am going to encourage you to listen to your own instincts, to look at your own family values, to question the expert advice, even mine, if it doesn't fit *your* child, and to question what the media is telling you about young people today.

As you will see, Affirming Parenting comes down to a few key points that I hope will appeal to your common sense:

• Love your children extravagantly, no matter their age.

- Be actively involved in their lives, but allow them to be children first.
- Share your family values.
- Set limits and consequences for their behaviors.
- Help them make independent decisions.
- Enjoy this parenting time.

I'll talk about all of these throughout the book.

Let's get started.

CHAPTER 1

New Challenges and New Solutions

THERE IS NO QUESTION that children today are growing up in a different world from the one you grew up in. Most of you had married parents and a mom who didn't work outside the home. Society still viewed divorce as unacceptable; churches debated it with the same fervor now reserved for same-sex marriage. Today the divorce rate is 4 times higher than it was in 1960, affecting one million children each year. Twenty million children are growing up with only one parent in the home. In the 1960s, only 1 in 4 children had two parents who worked full-time. Today, more than 3 in 4 do, and many children and adolescents are coming home after school to empty houses.

We are marrying later and having children later. The average age of marriage is now twenty-six for women and twenty-seven for men, nearly six years older than it was for our parents' generation. The average age a woman has her first baby is at an all-time high: twenty-seven. In 1970, when some of today's parents were born, the average first-time mom was just over twenty-one. And we are having fewer children. On average, a woman born between 1930 and 1939 had three children; most of us are only having two. Men also begin parenthood later. Birth rates since 1980 have increased by 40 percent in men ages thirty-five to forty and decreased by 20 percent in men under age thirty. (Does maturity make us better parents or just more tired ones?)

Changing family patterns are not all that makes parenting in the twenty-first century a challenge. There is HIV/AIDS. Twenty-five sexually transmitted diseases. Date-rape drugs. Binge drinking. Attention deficit hyperactivity disorder. Pressures to succeed unknown to earlier Americans. Ubiquitous sports leagues that start in preschool. Changing gender roles. Oral sex, "hooking up," and "friends with benefits." The Internet and MySpace Web pages. No wonder parents feel overwhelmed.

THE INFLUENCE OF TODAY'S MEDIA

One of the most dramatic differences between today's parenting landscape and the one you grew up in is the virtual explosion of exposure to media. When I was a child, there were three national channels on the television and a handful of local AM radio stations; today we have hundreds of cable TV and satellite radio programs, and seemingly limitless exposure to media. Today's early adolescents may have access to a cell phone, text messaging, e-mail, the Internet in their bedroom, televisions with more than a hundred channels, iPods, BlackBerries, and personal organizers. Often, the parents know much less about this technology than their children do. It's not uncommon for homes to have multiple computers, multiple television sets, and multiple private cell phones, and for family members to retreat to separate parts of the house to use them alone. I grew up in a house with one telephone line and one television set, which we watched together in the basement. How about you?

Nor did we have a news media feeding us the latest stories of child kidnappings, bombings, and natural disasters twenty-four hours a day. It's hard to remember that CNN's twenty-four-hour news coverage debuted in 1980 and was seen as a bold experiment.

I believe that this constant source of bad news contributes to the heightened anxiety we feel for our children. Today's parents seem to worry from the moment their children are born. Fears about SIDS become fears of child abductions by strangers, which become fears of AIDS, pregnancies, online predators, and school shootings. Yet, as we will see in coming chapters, kidnappings are not up, school shootings are rare, and teen pregnancies are near their lowest rates ever. The difference is that as parents we hear about them more; an Amber Alert about a missing child in Nevada shows up on my computer in Connecticut within minutes of being reported. In chapters 3 through 9, I will ask you to test your "fear factor." These short quizzes will help you determine which of your fears for your child are truly things to be concerned about and which are false fears created by media stories.

The tragedy of 9/11 has also left us feeling less secure about our children's future. Author Jodi Picoult wrote an essay about the impact of 9/11 on parenting her children in which she said: "Before 9/11, I had a much better handle on parenting. I knew what was safe and what was not...I worried on my children's behalf about bullies and cliques and the day the cafeteria served fun fish shapes for lunch—not about anthrax and smallpox and wars half a world away. After 9/11, however, I got scared...I found myself lying to my own children. I told them they were safe, when the truth was, I was not entirely sure." But neither were parents sure during World War II, the cold war, or the Vietnam War. There is a difference, though: those parents may have watched the evening news for a half hour in the early evening. Period. Today, most of us get news updates every time we check our e-mail.

My hope is that, after reading this book, the next time you see a news report that has bad news about children or teens—obesity, drug use, kidnappings, and so on—rather than panic, you will ask yourself how much of this is really true, how it may affect your family, and how you can use the news report to create a "teachable moment" to talk with your children about healthy behaviors.

THE GOOD NEWS FOR PARENTS TODAY

The landscape for twenty-first-century parents is undeniably challenging, but there is a lot of good news for parents today. For instance, relationships between most parents and children have changed for the better. Although we are working more hours than our own parents did, we are actually spending more time with our children—more time teaching, playing with, and caring for our children—than our parents did. Fathers today spend nearly triple the time on child care than their fathers did, and Gen X dads spend an average of one hour more a day with their children than boomer dads.

A more subtle positive change has been happening as well. Barbara Levi-Berliner, a social worker and parenting expert, calls it the "democraticization" of the American family. Remember the family of 1950s television? There was even a program called *Father Knows Best*. Ward Cleaver and Jim Anderson were the heads of their households. Their wives wore aprons and high heels and did not work outside the home. When Dad came home from work, the family welcomed him with kisses and dinner. A frequent reprimand from Mom was, "Wait until your father gets home." In some shows, like *My Three Sons, Family Affair*, and *Full House*, there was not even a need for Mom; she had died of some unspecified disease before we ever met the family.

Compare that to parents on today's shows, like *Medium, The O.C., Seventh Heaven, Veronica Mars*, and *Gilmore Girls*. These parents involve their children in decision making about important issues and struggle to maintain a balance between helping their children become independent and protecting them when necessary. For the best parenting on television, in my opinion, you'll need to turn to a two-decades-old sitcom on Nick at Nite. *The Bill Cosby Show*, featuring the Huxtable family, is one of the best fictional examples I know of healthy parenting and family styles. Both parents worked, family dinner was common, and parents negotiated important decisions and limit setting with their children.

We also have more tools and knowledge to face challenges than other generations of parents. Our children are healthier than any other generation of children in history. We have more than forty years of research on parenting showing us that finding the balance between nurturing our children's growing independence and setting limits and consequences for their behaviors, a style I call Affirming Parenthood, is most effective at raising responsible and healthy children and teenagers. We also have new sophisticated research on how the adolescent brain develops, which helps us know how to improve the chances that our tweens and teens will effectively cope with risk taking. We have insights from the social sciences, such as the pioneering work of Daniel Goleman, to help us understand the concept of "emotional intelligence." We have access to medications that when properly used and prescribed, can help some children with learning disabilities learn and cope more effectively.

And as a result of our improved parenting, our children and teenagers are behaving more responsibly than have recent generations of young people. In fact, on almost every indicator of risk-taking behavior, tweens and teens today behave much more conservatively than their older brothers and sisters. The U.S. Centers for Disease Control and Prevention has conducted an annual survey of risk-taking behaviors among middle school and high school–age youth since 1991. Although it's true that some youth are engaging in risky behavior that could compromise their future and their health, in comparing the behaviors of teens in 2005 (the latest year for which statistics are available) with teens in 1991 (the first year of the study),

- Lifetime and current alcohol use are down, and binge drinking is down.
- Cigarette and other tobacco use is down.
- Teen pregnancy rates, teen birth rates, teen STD rates, and teen abortion rates are down. So are teen rates of sexual intercourse.
- Teen condom use is at its highest rate ever.
- High school dropout rates are down.
- Rates of teens committing crimes—including homicide, rape, violent crime, and violent deaths—are all down. Fewer teens have even been in a physical fight compared to fifteen years ago.

Only marijuana use is up compared to 1991, and it has been decreasing since 1999. So has adolescent use of cocaine, Ecstasy, and hallucinogenic drugs.

According to sociologist Dr. Michael Males, who studies trends among young people, "teenage girls…are far safer today than girls of twenty and thirty years ago. Teenage binge drinking has dropped 25% since 1970, smoking declined 20 to 50% depending on the measure, and drunken driving deaths are down 40%."

Today's children and youth offer new hope for the future. In their book, *Millennials Rising: The Next Great Generation*, Neil Howe, William Strauss, and R. J. Matson named the generations of children born after 1982 as the Millennial Generation. Their research showed that compared to other generations of young people, these children, teens, and young adults are closer to their parents, more respectful of their parents' values, more likely to recognize the importance of education and community service, and more respectful of cultural norms. They are more likely to reject stereotypes by sex, race, gender, or sexual orientation.

Overall, today's children and youth feel good about themselves. In a study of children aged eight to eighteen in 2003 by the Kaiser Family Foundation, 88 percent of young people report that they have lots of friends and 75 percent say that they are happy at school. Only a quarter say that they get in trouble a lot, with fewer than 1 in 10 saying that sounds a lot like them.

We must be doing something right. Indeed, a Public Agenda 1999 survey found that three-quarters of teens trust their parents to be there for them, and the Kaiser Family Foundation found that 86 percent of teens said that they get along well with their parents. Some of us may have grown up at a time when there was a saying, "Don't trust anyone over thirty," but that is not a slogan that resonates with our children. In a study of high school students, more than three-quarters said that having a close family relationship was important. My own twenty-two-year-old daughter and I share much more than I did with my mother when I was twenty-two. She's never heard of the saying, and doesn't relate to it at all. Today's adolescents and young adults value their parents, their teachers and professors, and their older friends.

WHAT WE CAN DO BETTER

The research bears out that we are doing many things right as parents today, and our children are benefiting. But as I talk to parents around the country, I have found that along with our increased involvement in our children's lives come some perhaps unintended consequences, in particular three that may compromise effective parenting. Here are some things we can do better:

1. Be parents first, friends second.

Many of today's parents want to be friends with their children, almost at any cost. They worry about setting limits and being unpopular with their children. They worry that their children are not popular enough. A woman called me recently, concerned about the amount of drinking at teenage parties. I asked whether the parties were chaperoned, and she said that they often weren't or that the parents stayed in another part of the house. When I suggested to her that her teenage children only be allowed to attend parties where she had verified that an adult would be home, she said her son would be mortified if she made such a call. She went on to say that teens don't think it's a party if there are chaperones present. Exactly. But she was unwilling to risk making her fifteen-year-old son unhappy. Ironically, some of these same parents who permit their middle school and high school teens to go to unchaperoned parties worry that their children will experiment with alcohol, drugs, and sex too early.

Often mothers have said to me proudly, "My daughter is my best friend." I am delighted that Alyssa and I are close and connected now that she is a young adult, but she certainly did not consider me her best friend in high school. She often complained that I was the "strictest progressive parent" among all her friends. It was very clear in our home that her dad and I were her parents first, her friends second. I did not enjoy making her sad or angry when I told her "no" when she wanted to do something I didn't think she was ready for or thought was inappropriate, but I could tolerate her not liking me for the moment—or even for a few days. I can't begin to count the number of times I said something like, "It's okay that you're angry with me right now. Sometimes I need to make decisions that you won't like but that will keep you safe. That's my job as your mom. We can be friends when you are grown up."

There was a woman at one of my talks who epitomized for me the parent who wanted her child to think she was cool. This mom asked me what to do about her seven-year-old daughter who wanted to wear midriff tops and low-rise jeans. I started to explain about the importance of helping her daughter understand that certain clothes were for grownups only, and that she could offer her daughter a choice of clothes from appropriate stores or mail-order catalogs, then she interrupted me. "But I don't want to destroy her fashion sense," she said, "and I don't want her to be mad at me."

I keep coming into contact with parents who are afraid to set limits, afraid to seem "uncool," afraid to make their children unhappy with them, even temporarily. But you will see that children do better when we are willing to act like their parents, to set limits, and to follow through on consequences. They want us involved in their lives, and they want to know our values.

2. Treat your children's accomplishments as theirs—not yours.

This may be the first generation of parents who look to their children to validate their own accomplishments. In fact, many of today's parents view their children's accomplishments somehow as being their own, with the grand prize being admission to a prestigious college or university.

Garrison Keillor's radio program *A Prairie Home Companion* describes Lake Wobegon as a place where "all the children are above average." For many parents, that phrase might be "all the children are extraordinary." A woman in a well-to-do suburb outside Boston confided in me, "We joke about the fact that we want our children to have straight As: they should all be Attractive, Academic, Artistic, and Athletic." I am struck by how many parents tell me that their children are "gifted"; how hard it seems to be for parents to accept that their children might just be average and that that's okay.

Perhaps this increased emphasis on our children's achievements is because many people are having children later in life and having fewer children than their parents did. As a result, they tend to treat their children with a sense of greater preciousness and importance. There was a woman in my new mother's group in her early forties who had just had her first child. When we were introducing ourselves and our babies, she said, "This is Hannah, but I should call her 'Basket.' We looked at her, puzzled. She explained: "Because I had her so late, we're putting all our eggs in her." We laughed, but I wonder whether that might not be true for many thirtysomething parents, too.

This is perhaps also the first generation of parents who look to their children to give meaning to their lives. That places a big burden on them. Other generations of parents wanted their children to grow up, move out, make a living, get married, and have children. We want all that, but we also want our children to be fulfilled and to fulfill us. How often I hear my friends and the parents at my talks say, "My children are everything to me." Our children are trying desperately to measure up.

3. Emphasize happiness before success.

Ask yourself honestly for a moment, "Would I rather my child be successful or happy?" I am guessing you answered, "Happy, of course." In counseling sessions, when I ask parents what they want for their children, they often say, "I just want them to be happy." In a 2006 *Redbook* poll, when asked about their "single biggest concern for your children," readers put their children's happiness at the top of the list, closely followed by safety, health, and having the morals to "grow up to be good people." But, in doing research for this book, I asked the question, "What are your primary roles and responsibilities as a parent?" Hundreds replied, and only two people wrote "to help my child grow up happy."

Actions speak louder than words. In subtle and perhaps not so subtle ways, many of us are giving our children the message that being accomplished is more important than being happy—or perhaps that being successful is the key to happiness. Ask your children which they think you want for them. You might be surprised.

After a recent sermon in which I discussed valuing happiness over success, a congregant asked me, "But aren't they related? Can't I hope that my child is both happy and successful?" Of course. It's a matter of emphasis.

Various anthropologists, theologians, and psychologists have studied what makes people happy. They have discovered that happy people report a sense of belonging, responsibility to others, challenge, friendship, love, pleasure, confidence, and security in their lives. A study of students in Missouri and South Korea found that in both countries, despite their disparate cultures, people were happy when they had the same things: a feeling of connection, competence, and self-esteem. Parents should do all they can to make sure those things are in place in their children's lives.

WHAT ARE YOUR HOPES FOR YOUR CHILDREN?

What do you hope for your children when they reach adulthood? Yes, happiness, but what else? Take a minute to think about or, better yet, write down ten words you would like to be able to use to describe your son or daughter on high school graduation day—or what words you would like them to use to describe themselves.

1. _____

2. _____

3. _____

4. _____

5. _____

6. _____

7. _____

8. _____

9. _____

10. _____

Here are some words that parenting experts use to describe "good kids":

> honest
> self-reliant
> kind
> cooperative
> cheerful
> intellectually curious
> achievement-oriented
> socially accepted
> well behaved
> empathic
> caring
> compassionate
> moral
> funny.

Here are some of the skills they mention:

> ability to establish and maintain friendships
> involvement in extracurricular activities
> strong verbal and communication skills
> problem-solving and perspective-taking skills
> doing well in school
> appreciated at home, at school, and in the community.

What else is on *your* list? Parenting is a long-term commitment. What is the end result you would like to have? As with other important parts of life, it often helps if you know when you start out, at least vaguely, where you would like to end up. Your answers will partially depend on your values, culture, family situation, and the hopes your parents had for you.

My own shorthand answer is that I would like my children to enjoy their lives and have a sense of purpose. I hope they find their passion in the world and follow it. I hope they find partners and friends who love them fully and unconditionally and whom they love back. I hope that they will leave their adolescent years without any lifelong scars or irreversible mistakes.

What can we do to achieve our hopes?

We can use the research about how to effectively parent children and adolescents so that they grow up to be productive, happy, and independent adults. In the next chapter I will share with you nearly forty years of research on parenting styles and introduce you to the Affirming Parent.

CHAPTER 2

Affirming Parents

GOLDILOCKS FOUND that one bed was too hard, one bed was too soft, and one was just right. One bowl of porridge was too hot, one was too cold, and one was just right. Dr. Bob Selverstone, a psychologist who specializes in teens and families, first suggested to me that parents face the same Goldilocks search for "just right" in raising our children: we want to be neither too strict nor too permissive, neither too protective nor too hands-off, neither too involved nor too distant. Fortunately, today we have the benefit of decades of parenting research to help us get it just right.

How you approach parenting can either increase your chances of having a "good kid" or increase the odds that you and your children will struggle greatly on their journey to adulthood. The seminal work on how parenting styles affect children appeared more than forty years ago. A young researcher named Diana Baumrind at the University of California at Berkeley published a paper in the journal *Child Development* in 1966 that outlined four distinct parenting types. She said that the two most important characteristics that defined these styles were "parental responsiveness"—how warm and supportive parents are—and "parental demandingness," or how parents try to influence behavior, supervise, and discipline their children.

Her model on parenting styles forms the basis for most parenting research to this day. Research results about how these styles affect children from diverse ethnic and income levels have been remarkably consistent over the years. Ann Hulbert, in her survey of one hundred years of parenting advice books, *Raising America*, writes that all the books struggle with the questions "How much power and control do, and should, parents wield over a child's journey from dependence to independence? How much freedom and autonomy do children need, or want, along the way?"

Throughout each stage of your child's life you will try to strike the right balance between being nurturing and being in charge, between letting your child take chances and face the consequences and guiding him or her away from what you think are the wrong choices. You faced this when your toddler climbed on the furniture. You face it now in deciding whether your child is ready to walk to school alone or go to the mall with friends. You'll face it when your child is applying to college or choosing where to live. The situations change, but the challenge remains the same: How do we get the parenting balance just right?

WHAT KIND OF PARENT ARE YOU?

Before reading about the different parenting styles, spend a minute on this quiz. Read the four statements and choose which one most closely resembles how you approach your children. Don't take a long time to think this through; go with your first instinct. (Would your children agree with your answer about your style?)

DECISION MAKING
a. My children ask my opinion, but generally they make their own decisions.
b. I make most decisions for my children without asking their opinions.
c. I ask my children for their opinions, but I make most important decisions.
d. I let my children make their own decisions.

CHORES

a. My children help out in our home only when they
want to.
b. My children have a list of chores that they must complete
each week. I assign the tasks.
c. My children have chores to do each week, and we
frequently work together to complete them.
d. My children have no chores and responsibilities in our
household.

MONITORING

a. I do not monitor my children's homework; that's their
responsibility.
b. I check my children's homework each night against their
list of assignments.
c. I am available to help my children with their homework if
they ask, and I check in with them each day to see that
tomorrow's work is ready.
d. I do not care about how my children do in school; in the
long run, it doesn't matter.

CONSEQUENCES

If my sixteen-year-old came home after a night of drinking,
I would:
a. Ignore it; teens drink.
b. Ground him or her for a month.
c. Talk to him or her about it and go over our house rules
about alcohol.
d. I probably wouldn't know; I don't wait up for my children.

DISCIPLINE

When my three-year-old throws food in a restaurant, I
a. Distract her with a toy or DVD.
b. Yell at her, "Stop it now!"
c. Ask her to help me clean it up and then tell her if she does
it again, we will need to leave the restaurant.
d. Ignore her.

SETTING LIMITS

When my twelve-year-old asks to go to a boy/girl party, I

a. Say yes and drive my child there.

b. Say, "No, twelve is too young for such parties."

c. Call the parents where the party is to be held to make sure they are going to be home to chaperone, and talk with my child about my expectations.

d. Say yes and tell him to get a ride.

THE FOUR PARENTING STYLES

The four parenting styles are known by parenting researchers as Permissive, Authoritarian, Authoritative, and Uninvolved/ Neglectful. All four styles are considered to be "normal" styles of parenting.

Permissive

If you chose more "A's" than anything else, you are probably a "Permissive" Parent. Permissive Parents tend to be more responsive to their children's needs than demanding. Permissive Parents regularly consult with their children, give lots of explanations for their decisions, and allow their children to basically decide their own behaviors. Although close to their children, they make few demands on them for conformity, orderly behaviors, or chores. This is the parent who lets a preschooler strew toys all over the living room and leave them there. This is the parent who lets adolescent children leave the house without knowing where they are going, who asks where they went when they return but without much comment, and who involves their children in all family decisions. Such parents may look the other way when their teens come home after drinking and may allow their teens to have sex with a boyfriend or girlfriend in their homes. Their slogans might be "Boys will be boys" and "That's what teenagers do."

Authoritarian

If you chose more "B's" than anything else, you are probably an "Authoritarian" Parent. Authoritarian Parents reverse the permissive approach: they are more demanding of their children than responsive to their needs. They set clear rules and boundaries, and often hold their children to an absolute standard of conduct. They tend to be harsher in their discipline. These are the parents who select which toys their preschooler plays with at a specific time, insist the child put those toys away, and often rely on "because I said so" as the explanation for rules. These are the parents of an adolescent who tell him or her never to drink, smoke, or have sex because there will be dire consequences. They set curfews without engaging their teen children in the decision, and they punish them severely when curfews are not met. Their slogans might be "Just say no," "Do as I say," and "Because I'm the parent—that's why."

Affirming

If you chose more "C's" than anything else, you are probably what the parenting experts have labeled "Authoritative." I have renamed this style the "Affirming" Parent to avoid confusion with the "Authoritarian" style and to broaden the concept: I want to emphasize the idea of "affirming" all that is wonderful about your child. It's vital to affirm children's self-worth, to affirm their importance not only in your life but in the world at large, and to affirm the special qualities that each of them has to offer.

Affirming Parents are both nurturing and firm. They run their families as a "limited democracy." They love their children extravagantly, but it is clear that they are in charge. They are equally demanding and responsive. They set clear standards for their children's behaviors, but offer explanations for these standards and are open to give-and-take with their children about what the standards for present and future conduct should be. They affirm their child's good qualities. They are actively involved in their children's and teens' lives but allow their children age-appropriate independence. They probably sit down to play with their children with their toys and help them clean them up until all is put back. As the parent of an adolescent, they jointly agree upon a time for curfew and what the consequences will be if curfew is missed. They share with their children their values about drinking and sex, but also tell them to call if they need a ride and to use birth control and condoms if they do have sexual intercourse. Their children have chores that they are expected to do as members of the family. Rather than using psychological control, they seek to give their children opportunities to develop their own thoughts and feelings and the skills to express them. One might call these Goldilocks parents: neither too strict nor too permissive, they seek to get it "just right."

Uninvolved

A parent who chose mostly "D's" might be considered "Neglectful" or "Uninvolved." Not many of these parents are likely to be taking the time to read this book. These parents are low in responsiveness and demandingness, although not rejecting or abusive of their children. They live in parallel universes with their children and become involved only when they have to. Their children are not expected to help out around the home, nor do they check in much with their parents when they are adolescents.

While they aren't considered abusive, in my mind Uninvolved Parents leave their children feeling insecure and unwanted. As you'll see, the effects can be lifelong.

IMPACT OF THE FOUR PARENTING STYLES

In more than forty years of research, parenting style has been found to make a difference in children's lives, regardless of income level or ethnic background. Overall, children of Affirming Parents generally do best on any number of indicators. The impact of Authoritarian and Permissive Parenting styles is remarkably similar. Dr. Baumrind predicted this nearly forty years ago. In 1966, she wrote: "Demands which cannot be met or no demands, suppression of conflict or sidestepping of conflict, refusal to help, or too much help, unrealistically high or low standards, all may curb or understimulate the child so that he fails to achieve the knowledge and experience" he or she needs to succeed.

Children of Affirming Parents tend to have fewer problem behaviors from toddler age through adolescence and into young adulthood. They are the least likely to smoke, drink, binge drink, or use drugs, and they experience fewer school problems and delin-quent behaviors. They are more socially competent and have fewer psychological problems. They are less likely to begin sexual inter-course early and less likely to become pregnant as teenagers. Like children of Authoritarian Parents, they do well in school (as meas-ured by grade point average), are unlikely to use drugs, and have low involvement in such behaviors as shoplifting, stealing, and commu-nity pranks. Like children of Permissive Parents, they score high in self-reliance and social competence.

Authoritarian Parenting has positive outcomes on certain vari-ables, but at a cost to the child. These children generally do well in school and engage in fewer risk-taking behaviors as adolescents. In other words, they are less likely to drink, use drugs, or engage in delinquent behaviors. But they have lower self-esteem, higher levels of depression, and poorer self-concept than other children. In fact, on scales related to positive self-concept, children from Authoritarian homes tend to do no better than children from Neglectful homes. And the more parents try to control their adoles-cents' behaviors, the more likely their children are to take dangerous risks as young adults when they are finally allowed to be out on their own. Indeed, parents who use psychological control over their chil-dren and teenagers often harm children's developing sense of self. Criticizing children, making them feel shame or guilt, and fighting and arguing instead of trying to mutually solve problems often result in children who feel unloved and unworthy.

Children with Permissive Parents represent the flip side of this picture. They are indeed risk takers, as those with an Authoritarian bent might fear. They do less well in school and are more likely to use alcohol and tobacco, more likely to get involved in sexual inter-course early, and more likely to misbehave in school. On problem behaviors, they do no better than children from Neglectful or Uninvolved homes. But the strong support they get from their par-ents has a positive payoff, as does their control of their own decision making. These young people have higher levels of self-esteem, strong self-confidence, and lower levels of depression. They may act out, but they feel good about themselves when they do! They may be hellions as adolescents, but if they survive intact, they do well as adults—although problems associated with risk-taking behaviors tend to persist into early adulthood.

Children of Uninvolved Parents are the most blatant risk takers as adolescents, are much more likely to experience depression, and have the lowest self-esteem. And these effects continue throughout life. In a national study of adults ages twenty-five to seventy-four, researcher Benjamin Shaw and colleagues found that "a lack of parental support during childhood is associated with increased levels of depressive symptoms and chronic conditions in adulthood."

We begin using these different parenting styles almost from our children's first days. During the toddler and preschool years, these styles tend to emerge with greater clarity. As any of us with children older than age two know, toddlers and preschoolers are tough. I adored the stage of parenthood from six months to eighteen months. These children are discovering something new about themselves and the world each day; they teach us to delight in the everyday acts of living. But at about the age of eighteen months, children learn the word *no*. They learn that they have some ability to control what they want in their environment. They test limits on a regular basis. They can start having tantrums when their will is thwarted by the grownups in their lives. Some of them temperamentally can be very willful.

There are many good books about raising toddlers and preschoolers, so I won't go into specifics here. The point I want to make is that how we respond as parents to our toddlers and preschoolers begins to make a difference in how they will be in the world as they grow older. Even at ages three and four, an Affirming Parenting style pays off.

Think about this situation for a moment. You are in a restaurant with your three-year-old, who is in a high chair. The food is late in coming. He is getting crankier by the minute. The food finally arrives, and with a sweep of his hand, he dumps the plate on the floor and starts to wail. The Permissive Parent is likely to order a second dinner and assume he'll quiet down eventually. The Authoritarian Parent might smack his hand and tell him he'll have to sit there without food while the adults finish. The Affirming

Parent would likely pick him up and take him out of the restaurant, have the other parent get the food to go, and feed him at home. Even more important, the Affirming Parent would have talked with him about good restaurant behavior before the visit and what would happen if he misbehaved.

There are many other ways to handle this kind of situation. The research tells us that what is most important is to be consistent and kind in our discipline. It is harsh and inconsistent handling of these early oppositional behaviors that can cause problems later on. Parents who are harsh and inconsistent with discipline often confuse children about how to manage their own behavior. Parents may become increasingly coercive in their discipline, or if the misbehavior seems frequent, they may become increasingly inconsistent about when and whether they discipline and monitor at all. The child never knows whether consequences will be carried out, and the aggressive behavior may become more established.

By the time these children enter kindergarten, they may be difficult to manage and slow to self-soothe. (Some children, though, will thrive in a classroom that can offer the fair and firm discipline they are not getting at home.) These children are often in trouble with the teacher, and their classmates prefer not to play with them. Because of this, they may do less well in school. By early adolescence, they may seek out other young people who are also more likely to be difficult or rejected, and become involved in a peer group that turns to alcohol or drugs or other risk-taking behaviors to feel better about themselves. In high school, risk-taking behaviors increase, and they may become teenagers who have a whole host of problems. (If you already feel you have a preschooler or elementary school child who has these kinds of behavior problems, this is the time to get help. Studies show that treating what psychologists call "conduct disorder" in childhood, when the problems first arise, and getting support for your own parenting practices can make the difference between a well-adjusted teenager and one who is in repeated trouble. See the Appendix for ideas on where to find help.)

It's not that difficult to imagine what happens to preschoolers as they become tweens and adolescents if discipline and monitoring remain inconsistent. Picture the eleven-year-old who is punished for a bad report card but whose parents don't look over homework assignments, or the teen who comes home drunk and the parents ignore it, or the ninth grader who is grounded sometimes when her chores are not done and other times has no consequences for the same behavior. Young people who can't count on their parents' consistent reinforcing of consequences when they ignore agreed-upon limits are much more likely to keep testing them.

Before we begin discussing what it means to be an Affirming Parent, I'd like you to do another exercise. How would you complete this sentence?

My primary responsibilities as a parent are:

_____

_____

_____

I asked parents at focus groups and through the Internet to fill in this sentence. I received hundreds of responses, no two of them exactly the same. Many parents answered a variation of "love them, love them, love them." Several parents mentioned being a good role model so that children could learn by example how "well-rounded, healthy, productive, and ethical adults behave." Several mentioned protecting children and preparing them for life. Here are some other answers:

- To give my children a secure home emotionally and financially.
- To keep my child safe, healthy, and educated.
- To try to give my child a sense of self-confidence and curiosity.
- To assist my children to grow into kind and caring adults.

One person said to "allow her to fail, and to provide a warm, safe place to land." Similarly, one mom wrote "to guide them through obstacles and teach them to deal with adversity." Many parents mentioned raising children who would find their passions and contribute to society or make the world a better place.

Let's look at the basic Affirming Parenting skills for how to put all this into practice.

THE SIX TOOLS OF THE AFFIRMING PARENT

Affirming Parenthood comes down to six key tools. There are lots of other "tips" that could be added to this list, but I think they all derive from these six.

1. Love your children unconditionally.

You may remember that one of the Ten Commandments is to "honor your father and mother." Frankly, I wish Moses had returned from the mountaintop commanding us to love our children, too. (That he did not is a reflection of how differently children were viewed three thousand years ago in the desert. The penalty in the Torah for not respecting parents is death by stoning. Yes, times have changed!)

Dr. Urie Bronfenbrenner, a renowned psychologist and a co-founder of the U.S. National Head Start program, is credited with the statement that children need an enduring, reciprocal, and irrational relationship with at least one person. In other words, what children need most are parents who are crazy about them, who love their children "more than anything and anyone." One parent I spoke to said that his primary role was to "love his children in extremis." The Search Institute, a research organization that studies children and families, says that children thrive when they are cherished as unique and irreplaceable.

When my children were preschoolers, we made up an "I love you more than" game that we still use today. One of us begins, "I love you more than all the stars in the skies." The other answers, "I love you more than all the sand on the beach," and we go from there. When he was three, Greg told me, "I love you more than all the ketchup at all the McDonald's in the world." That meant a lot.

But according to my colleague and social worker Barbara Levi-Berliner, parents need to understand that there is a difference between children knowing that they are loved and believing that they are lovable. Most children know that their parents love them, but they may not know that they are worthy people who will be loved by others. As one teen said to me, "Of course, my parents love me. They have to. I just don't think someone else ever will." We'll talk more about how to develop your child's sense of self-worth in several of the upcoming chapters.

2. Stay actively involved in your children's and teenagers' lives.

The most important advice I can give parents as their children move from childhood through adolescence is to stay involved in their daily lives. Parents of smaller children do this naturally, but it takes more effort as our children develop friendships apart from us, join activities outside of school and the faith-based institution, and later begin to drive. One parent of a fifteen-year-old girl plaintively asked me, "When are we going to talk if she does not need me to drive her from place to place anymore?"

Too many parents, as their children approach middle school and then high school, begin to pull back from active involvement. It's as if they feel they are "done" with active parenting. You are not done—probably ever, and certainly not until your child is launched into adulthood. Our tweens and teens need us. I am always surprised that fewer parents of middle schoolers and high schoolers than elementary school parents come to my talks on sexuality issues; it almost seems they have "given up" their opportunities for influence.

Do you remember this TV message from our youth: "It's ten p.m. Do you know where your children are?" Affirming Parents know where their children and teens are, whom they are with, and what they are doing. They provide crucial monitoring and supervision of their activities but do not spy on them. They seek opportunities to be with their children and for family engagement.

Think for a moment. How much do you know about your tweens' and teens' lives? Can you name their best friend? Do you know whom they eat lunch with? Do you know their favorite teacher?

Their favorite book? When was the last time you watched their favorite TV program with them? What Internet sites do they visit? Do they have a Web page or blog—and, if so, have you visited it?

The balancing act here is to stay involved but not so involved that you micromanage their lives or keep them from developing their own sense of independence and decision making. Our generation of parents, as you will read in chapter 4, has been dubbed the "helicopter" or even "hovercraft" parents. It is indeed hard to get it just right—just the right amount of involvement, neither benign neglect nor overbearing presence. Remember, you are not seeking to be your children's best friend, however appealing that may sound to you. You want them to enjoy being with you, but you also want them to begin to develop lives of their own.

The many young adults today who return to their families rather than move into the world of independent adulthood have been referred to as "adultolescents." The 2000 Census found that more than half of twenty-one to twenty-four-year-olds and a third of twenty-five to thirty-four-year-olds are still living at home or have returned to live in their parents' home more than once since college graduation. The National Opinion Research Center found that the average American believes adulthood now begins at twenty-six. The movie *Failure to Launch* featured an attractive thirtysomething man still living at home with his parents, who contract with an attractive thirtysomething woman to get him to move out. Let's hope none of us will have to resort to that! We can maintain a closeness with our children into adulthood while also nurturing their eventual independence. We can help them learn to make smart choices on their own through Affirming Parenting.

Forming a sense of independence is a critical developmental task during adolescence. I often remind parents of teens who are pulling away of this adage: "During childhood you were the hammer. Now you are the anvil." As Dr. Selverstone says, "You can let your children walk away from you, but you should always be there steadfast when they are ready to return."

Your job is to help your children learn to make good decisions on their own without your input. It would be lovely if every time our children faced an important decision they would come to us first. "Mom, I am thinking about having sex with Susan. What do you think?" "Dad, my friends are drinking at parties. I'd like to join them. Would that be okay with you?" Of course, we hope that our older children will want to discuss their big decisions like college and careers with us, but it is our job, in the words of the CDC parenting experts, to "respect and access the reasoning skills of children and help them develop their own sense of what is responsible behavior.... Media literacy, improved communication skills, strong problem-solving skills, and the ability to resist persuasive influences can support youth in their decision making and ability to cope."

3. Set limits jointly.

When I told my friend Ledell Mulvaney, a music teacher, about this book, she said, "Please talk to parents about limit setting and setting consequences. I have way too many students in my class who are out of control and desperately need parents who will be parents. Third graders tell me that they're watching movies like *The Terminator* while their parents read the paper in the other room."

Authoritarian Parents make the rules. Permissive Parents often have few, if any. Affirming Parents approach their families as a "limited democracy"—when their children are small, they define many of the parameters; but as they get older, they involve them in setting limits and consequences.

I believe that young people want our help and our parameters about their acceptable behavior. I think about several smaller children I knew who were whiny, demanding, and tantrum-prone. All had few limits on their behaviors. As children get older, they continue to need our limits to feel safe, but they can also be involved in setting them.

Bedtimes can be negotiated, for example. Rules for TV and Internet use can be developed jointly. Asking your children to research issues and present their case can be empowering, and you may find your conflict resolves itself. For example, when Alyssa was sixteen, she wanted to have her belly button pierced. I asked her to research the risks online and to present them to her father and me.

After seeing pages upon pages of pictures of infected navels, she decided she was not interested after all.

4. Set consequences and follow through.

Setting and being consistent about consequences is one of the most important skills of the Affirming Parent and one of the hardest to do "just right." Talking with your children about what they think will be fair consequences when you set limits together lets them know in advance that you are firm about your expectations for their behaviors.

The parenting literature has talked about natural and logical consequences for more than thirty years. "Natural" consequences are those that are not controlled by the parent. If a child stays up too late, she'll be tired the next day. If he skips dinner because he doesn't like what's being served, he'll be hungry at bedtime. If she goes outside without gloves, her hands will be cold. If he doesn't study for a test, he gets a poor grade. Our parents called it "learning the hard way," and if you can tolerate the outcome for your children, it's a great way for them to learn. The hard part is knowing which consequences are okay for them to tolerate: failing one test may be a lesson; allowing them to fail a course and have to repeat a grade because we aren't regularly monitoring their homework is taking a consequence too far.

"Logical" consequences are more about discipline and parents determining the consequences. They're usually used when there aren't natural consequences. You and your children agree in advance to what the consequences will be if an agreement is violated, and then you make sure that you (and they) follow through. The teen who misses curfew does not get to go out the following weekend. The child who doesn't want dinner doesn't get to have dessert. The tween who goes on an Internet site that you have not approved loses Internet privileges for a period of time. The idea behind logical consequences is that they follow from the behavior; finding out that your child is texting messages during class means losing cell phone privileges, not losing TV time.

But sometimes it's hard to come up with logical consequences that make sense. What is the logical consequence for not doing your chore of emptying the trash? The natural consequence is trash all over the floor, but we don't want to live with that in our homes. So ignoring household chores that affect the whole family after being nicely reminded a few times might need a more generic consequence that flows from your child's actions: "no TV or computer time until the trash is taken out" may be the motivation that your child needs.

I have seen many parents who tell their children that there will be consequences, but then back-pedal because of the inconvenience of carrying them through. No car for a week means that you may have to drive them to school or their job if there is no public transportation. No cell phones mean that they have no easy way to call you. Having to go over each homework assignment with your procrastinating eighth grader means a half hour out of your evening when you could be doing something else. You get the picture. But if you do not follow through, your child or teen will quickly learn that your consequences are merely threats and can be ignored. Be sure you can live with what you agree upon.

Anticipating consequences from their parents can make a big difference in adolescent involvement in risk behaviors. For example, teens who do not think their parents will do anything if they drink alcohol are much more likely to do so. Teens who think that their parents are okay about teens having sex are more likely to engage. The converse is also true: teens who believe that their parents will apply consequences are more likely to avoid the behaviors in the first place.

It is sometimes hard to know what consequences to set and then to stick to them. I admit that I'm not always good at this, and my children would tell you that my husband and I are sometimes overly strict. Let me share a recent example that I struggled to figure out.

Mornings in our house used to end regularly with my losing my temper in order to get Greg up and moving. He is a night owl, and waking up at 6:30 a.m. to be at school at 7:25 a.m. for band is excruciating. It is not unusual for us to wake him up, only to go back upstairs fifteen minutes later and see that he has gone back to sleep.

At that point, it is hard for me not to raise my voice. And we repeat this scene morning after morning.

I hated beginning every morning with this tension, so I challenged myself to do it a different way. I sat down with Greg to negotiate a natural and logical consequence. We agreed that if he is not up and dressed and ready to go to school on time, he will be late and have to go to the office and deal with the school's consequences. He will also need to walk rather than get a ride from one of us. In other words, I have decided it is his problem. I asked him how I could help in the morning. He told me he needs me to check on him five minutes after I wake him up to make sure he is up, and to start getting his breakfast ready. I agreed, and so far it has been a lot calmer in our house in the morning. (Well, most mornings.)

5. Communicate your family's values.

All children need to know their families' values. It's important for you to impart *your* messages to *your* children. Views on sexuality, alcohol and drug use, appropriate media for young people, the role of religion in your family, even the value of physical exercise and time outdoors all vary from one family to another, and may vary from what I present in this book. In this information age, your child will learn facts about almost every area of life from school, the media, and their friends. But only you as the parent can teach your children about *your* family's views.

It begins with how we treat one another. I have a strong value that every person deserves to be treated with dignity and respect and affirm the biblical teaching "Love your neighbor as yourself." Those form the hallmarks of how I hope we behave to one another in our home. I am certainly not a perfect mother, nor is my family perfect; I am guessing you're not, either. I lose my temper at times with my children, and I do not always bring the best of myself to all our interactions, especially when I am stressed. But it is a goal for the members of our family always to strive to treat one another with dignity and respect.

I know that actions speak louder than words. (As James Baldwin wrote in *Nobody Knows My Name*, "Children have never been very good at listening to their elders, but they have never failed to imitate them.") I also know that I should not be "preaching" our family values to my children. My children need me to be their mom, not their minister. Instead, parents want to model the behaviors that we hope our children will adopt. It does no good to tell them to exercise and eat well if we do not; if we treat our partner with disrespect, they will learn more from this than from our admonitions about kindness.

In my sexuality books, I urge parents to look for "teachable moments" in which to give children a little information based on something that just happened. Teachable moments can be used for messages about anything from exercise, eating well, schoolwork, alcohol and drug use, and safety, to community service. Greg used to point to his watch when I began a teachable moment. "Mom," he'd say, "these are teachable moments, not teachable hours." Keep them short, and try to make them a dialogue. For example, "Honey, what do you think about your school removing junk food from the cafeteria?" Or, "In our family, we think that racist comments hurt people and should be challenged." "In our family, we think that..." is the beginning of a teachable moment to share your values.

6. Understand the world your child is growing up in.

In the old days, parents may have scoffed that their children had it easy because when their parents were small, they had to walk miles to school in the snow. But have you ever told your child about the good old days before computers or when there were only five channels to watch on TV? Or how we used to have to go outside to play because there weren't video games and DVDs?

Yes, our children are growing up in a different world, and rather than bemoan it, we can celebrate with them all that that brings. We are blessed by living not only in the Internet age, but also in a time when more and more children can grow up to reach their potential. When people idealize the United States of the 1950s, they often forget about its pervasive racism and sexism, about segregation and poverty, and about the invisibility of ethnic, religious, or sexual diversity. Although the twenty-first century must still confront many of those "isms," our children are growing up in a country with much greater respect for diversity than the one we grew up in.

We can either be afraid of this new world or we can embrace it, learn about it, and help our child set limits. For example, as I'll talk about in chapter 9, forbidding your fourteen-year-old to have a MySpace page when all her friends do is likely to result in her creating one at school or at a friend's house or else feeling isolated and unnecessarily controlled. Affirming Parents understand that it might be better to help define the limits for safe use of these types of sites and then appropriately monitor them.

We also need to remember that children and teens understand their world in different ways than we do. Research now proves that a child's brain processes information very differently from an adult's. We know so much about child development and the adolescent brain (see chapter 5), and our own common sense tells us that our children do not see things the same way we do. Remembering this, and trying to remember what it felt like when *you* were their age, can go a long way in helping to understand your children's feelings and behaviors.

My last piece of advice for the Affirming Parent is to enjoy this special time. Yes, there are days when parenting makes us stressed, worried, and crazy. I find it most difficult on the days when one of my children is ill or unhappy about something in their lives. I once heard this adage: "You are only as happy as your most unhappy child." That has certainly been true for me.

But overall I love parenting and I can't think of anything that I'm doing that is more important than nurturing and raising Alyssa and Gregory. We are blessed to be parenting at this particular time in history. Our children are healthier than any other generation has ever been—when it comes to their physical health, we actually have less to worry about than parents have for the past fifty years. Let me show you why.

TEST YOUR FEAR FACTOR

1. The percentage of children and youth who are over weight is just over:
   a. 15%.
   b. 25%.
   c. 50%.
   d. 75%.

2. Compared to when we were teenagers, family dinners are:
   a. More likely today.
   b. Less likely today.
   c. About as likely today.

3. Compared to 1981, children today are:
   a. More likely to play outdoors.
   b. Less likely to play outdoors.
   c. About as likely to play outdoors.

4. Compared to 1981, children are:
   a. More likely to be on a sports team.
   b. Less likely to be on a sports team.
   c. About as likely to be on a sports team.

5. The incidence of eating disorders is:
   a. Going up.
   b. Going down.
   c. About the same.

* * * * *
Answers: 1. a; 2. c; 3. b; 4. b; 5. c.

CHAPTER 3

Their Bodies, Their Selves: Raising Physically Healthy Children

I RECENTLY SPENT a day at a private school in an upscale California suburb. I met with administrators and teachers during the day and offered a program for parents in the evening. In one of my meetings, the social worker told me that the school was seeing an increasing number of girls under fifteen who might be anorexic. She said that eating-disordered behavior seemed to be increasing at the school, despite their emphasis on nutrition and the bowls of fresh fruit that were everywhere. That evening, when I addressed the parents in my size 10 pants, I couldn't help noticing that I was probably the heaviest mother in the room. The average dress size in their affluent community of fortysomething moms seemed to be a 2. No wonder their daughters were striving for thinness! In a world that exalts the celebrity of very thin young women like Nicole Richie, Paris Hilton, Lindsay Lohan, and the Olsen twins, it would indeed seem plausible that our daughters (and, increasingly, our sons) are at the highest risk ever for eating disorders.

But wait. Aren't we also in the middle of what newspaper headline after newspaper headline calls an obesity crisis? On the reality show *Honey, We're Killing the Kids*, overweight children are morphed into forty-year-old obese adults, courtesy of computer modeling. In the episodes I watched, the "aged" pictures not only had the boys appearing overweight, but also balding, pockmarked, unshaven, and in bad clothes by their fortieth birthdays. After the intervention (which included such benign advice as "no junk food," "have the boys do chores," and "have the parents quit smoking"), the morphed pictures showed attractive, well-dressed, clean-shaven, trim forty-year-old men. The overweight parents of the boys stand amazed that family outings and healthier eating could lead to such a difference thirty years later. I'm amazed, too.

FACT vs. FEAR

How can our children be getting fatter at the same time that we are spending all week and all weekend watching them in organized sports? Didn't I just read that parents are spending more money than ever to assure that their children get on the right teams, that parents are getting too competitive about the outcomes of their children's games, and that we no longer have time to eat together as a family partly because we're too busy cheering on one family member or another?

What are the facts about our children's health? And what does parenting have to do with any of it?

Healthier Than Ever

Here is some of the best news about being a parent today: in the United States and most of the developed world, children and teenagers are healthier than they have ever been. They are much healthier than children a hundred years ago and, on many indicators, healthier than we were at their age. Our children in general are taking fewer risks with their physical health than we did at their age.

For most of recorded history, and still in many parts of the world today, parents could not be sure their children would survive until their first birthday or that an infectious disease would not kill them before their teenage years. In biblical times, the average woman had five children in order to assure that two would survive to adulthood. Just a hundred years ago in the United States, 160 out of every 1,000 babies born died during the first year of life. The number of babies who do not live until the age of one is called the infant mortality rate. During the past fifty years, this rate in the

United States declined by 77 percent. According to the U.S. Centers for Disease Control and Prevention (CDC), the "declines in infant mortality over the past five decades have been linked to improved access to health care, advances in neonatal medicine, and public health education campaigns such as the 'Back to Sleep' campaign to curb fatalities caused by SIDS." In the United States today, only 7 babies of every 1,000 born will die in the first year of life.

Our children are projected to live longer than any other generation in history, too. In biblical times, women lived on average only until the age of twenty-five, and the life expectancy for men was age forty. Again, according to the CDC: "from the turn of the 20th century through 2002, life expectancy at birth increased from 48 to 75 years for men and from 51 to 80 years for women." Nutrition, housing, hygiene, and access to medical care have all contributed to these increased longevity rates.

Penicillin and vaccinations are part of the reasons for the dramatic declines in childhood deaths. I remember when Alyssa was about eight or nine, her pediatrician diagnosed her rash and sore throat as scarlet fever. I panicked, immediately recalling Beth in Louisa May Alcott's *Little Women*—the youngest of the four sisters, almost angelic, who died of scarlet fever as a young teenager. It was a very sad moment for me in the fifth grade. I had not thought about it until that moment in the doctor's office, but I was very scared to hear those words applied to my child. It turns out that today a simple dose of antibiotics generally cures scarlet fever and almost all other infections that used to kill children.

Some baby-boom readers may remember standing in long lines at their elementary schools for the polio vaccine. Polio killed and crippled children of our parents' generation. Since the polio vaccine went into widespread use in 1955, polio has now been eradicated in the United States and indeed in all but seven countries around the world. In 1979, smallpox was eradicated around the world. Today more than twelve childhood diseases have been completely eradicated. You may remember accounts of more than 20,000 pregnant women who had been exposed to rubella (what you may remember being called German measles) giving birth to children with deafness, blindness, mental retardation, and heart defects between 1964 and 1965. In 2003, in contrast, there were only seven cases of rubella in the United States.

Vaccinations are the main reason measles, mumps, and rubella have all but disappeared in this country. Recent outbreaks of measles and mumps have demonstrated the importance of immunizing children. In today's world, it is often travelers from other countries who are reintroducing these diseases into the United States, and children who have not been immunized are then at risk. For example, in 2006, an unvaccinated seventeen-year-old American girl contracted measles while on a church mission trip in Romania; she attended church the first day she got back and transmitted her measles to thirty-four other people. No one died, but three people needed to be hospitalized. According to Dr. Eileen M. Ouellette, president of the American Academy of Sciences, "It is vital that we continue to immunize our children against these preventable diseases or else they will return. Each of these diseases, after all, is just a plane ride away."

Our children are taller and more robust than any other generation, too. In 1894, Dr. L. Emmett Holt wrote what is generally recognized as the first book of child-rearing advice, *The Care and Feeding of Children*. He chronicled that the average ten-year-old boy was 52 inches tall and weighed 66 pounds. By 2002, the average ten-year-old boy had grown more than 3 inches taller and almost 20 pounds heavier; the average ten-year-old girl had grown to 56.4 inches and nearly 88 pounds. And it appears they are reaching puberty earlier. Should we be concerned, or is this a result of their being healthier than ever?

Growing Up Too Soon?

You may remember hearing of a study about a decade ago that found that the average age for girls to begin breast development had fallen to ten for white girls and nine for black girls, with many beginning as early as the third grade. Headlines blared THIRD-GRADE GIRLS SHOWING SIGNS OF PUBERTY. What those news stories often failed to report was that the earlier appearance of breast buds and pubic hair did not mean a decrease in the age it took to complete puberty; it just takes longer these days for children to complete the pubertal process. Although the average age of first periods, or menarche, dropped dramatically from a little more than 15 in 1860 (from a study of personal data found in Bibles) to 12.5 in 2004, it has dropped by only two months since 1963. In other words, your daughter may begin developing breast buds and pubic and under-arm hair before you did, but her first period is likely to come at a similar time.

The emergence of these other signs, known as secondary sex characteristics, however, means that you may need to give her information earlier than your mother gave it to you. These discussions probably need to begin by the end of second grade for girls and by fourth grade for boys—earlier if your pediatrician notes signs of puberty that you may have missed. Some parents tell me that they wait for the elementary school to teach their children about puberty, but unfortunately most schools don't do this until the latter part of the fifth grade. For many girls, it is more a history lesson than the education they need!

There is less reliable trend data on male pubertal development, but researchers believe that boys are probably beginning maturation slightly earlier as well. Data from England in 1970 found that, on average, boys began pubertal changes at 11.6 years and finished at 14.9. According to 2001 research in the United States, on average, boys are beginning puberty just past the age of 10 and finishing around 15.9 years. Genital growth for boys is beginning on average at about the age of 10. These data suggest that onset is earlier but completion is later. Another study found a drop of about three months in the past three decades in the onset of pubic hair development (which occurs at around age 12 for white boys and 11 for black boys.) Interesting: the last time a researcher studied the age of first ejaculation—which is the marker that would compare most directly with first menstruation—was the late 1940s. It was 14 then.

There are a variety of reasons that scientists offer to explain these decreases in age of onset of puberty. Almost all agree that the declining age of puberty compared to a hundred years ago is the result of better nutrition and better overall health. But some have raised the issue of whether there is something nefarious in the environment bringing about these changes, and there have been isolated cases in the scientific literature of children as young as five or six beginning puberty. Many people wonder whether pesticides or hormones in food are a cause.

We often use an online service to do our grocery shopping. One week, the man who delivered the groceries informed me that the store was out of organic milk. We buy organic milk primarily because Gregory finds that it tastes better. The deliveryman said to me, "We only buy organic milk, too. We read in the paper that the hormones in milk and meat are what's causing girls to get their periods earlier and earlier, and we don't want that for our nine-year-old daughter."

What are the facts? It turns out this is a hotly debated topic in endocrinology circles. Some people have raised concerns that soy-based infant formulas are responsible; some believe it is the result of hormones fed to cattle (known as "exogenous estrogens"); others believe that leakage from the plastic wrap that covers so much of our food is the culprit. A study of early pubertal development of girls in Puerto Rico found that girls with earlier breast development were exposed to the wastes from factories making oral contraceptives and plastics. Yet, in a review, two scientists concluded: "There are no published data to support the notion that an increased overall exposure to environmental estrogens has led to an increased incidence in precocious puberty or to an earlier start of pubertal development." In one comprehensive review of the century's long trend toward decreasing age at puberty, Dr. Robert Sprinkle, physician and professor at the University of Maryland, shares research that climate change and artificial lighting may actually be the most recent contributors to earlier pubertal changes. He writes that toxicity is "unlikely to assume a major role—an appearance here or there, but nothing steady."

We have reason to be concerned but not alarmed about early pubertal development, although there may not be much we as parents can do about it. Researchers have known for some time that girls who reach puberty earlier are more likely to begin sexual intercourse at younger ages. Substance abuse is more likely in earlier developing boys and girls. If your child reaches puberty at an early age, it may be especially important for you to read the sections in the next chapters on sex and substance use. Younger age at menarche is also a known risk factor for breast cancer in later life.

But does your child starting puberty earlier than you did warrant parental action or anxiety? Not in most cases. An average decrease of two or three months over the past thirty or forty years is not cause for alarm, especially because it is part of a decades-long trend toward earlier onset of puberty. If your son is starting to grow underarm or public hair before age nine or your daughter shows pubic hair or breast development before age seven, it should be checked out by your pediatrician—who is likely to refer your child for an evaluation by an endocrinologist, as a 1999 article in the prestigious journal *Pediatrics* recommends. (A general recommendation that we should all be following, according to the American Association of Pediatrics, is to make sure our children have an annual pediatric visit, or well-child exam, every year until the age of twenty-one, for a variety of reasons.) The use of monthly puberty-blocking injections is now becoming more common for early developers, but I recommend at least a second opinion before taking that course of action because of side effects. And as far as feeding your child organic milk, chicken, eggs, and beef—while that is certainly better for the animals involved and will reduce your child's exposure to the chemicals in cow feed, it is unlikely to change anything about your child's entrance into puberty.

One of the factors we do know that is correlated with pubertal development is a girl's weight—heavier girls get their periods earlier than thinner ones—and we all know that there is a childhood obesity crisis. Or is there?

Weighty Issues

Based on all the media stories on childhood obesity, I would have guessed that more than half the children in this country are overweight. The real answer surprised me: as measured by body mass index, 13 percent of high school students are considered over-weight. In 2003–04, 17 percent of children ages two to nineteen were overweight, according to the National Health and Nutrition Examination Survey, a governmental survey that goes back to the 1960s. In 1980, only 5 percent of children in that age range were overweight. You can see here how the presentation of statistics makes a difference in how dramatic this increase seems. Put a more reassuring way, more than 8 in 10 American children and teens are not overweight.

21st-CENTURY CHALLENGES

We do need to be concerned that nearly 1 in 5 children is over-weight, especially if it is one of our own children. Overweight children have an increased risk for high cholesterol and high blood sugar, which may be risk factors for adult heart disease. The much more immediate consequence for children is the social discrimination and stigma they may face if they are larger than their friends. And that's where you come in. It's important to talk to your children about healthy eating and exercise and, if your children are overweight, to be sensitive to how that affects them socially. One of my friends who was very overweight as a child says that he didn't need his mother to talk to him about being fat; he knew he was fat. What he needed was her ongoing support for how to deal with it. Research bears this out. In an article published in *Obesity* in October 2006, more than three thousand overweight adults were asked how they responded to their experiences of stigma and discrimination due to their weight. Almost everyone said they ate.

Distorted Self-Image

More young people perceive themselves to be overweight than actually are. Among high school students, nearly half report that they are trying to lose weight. Girls were twice as likely to be on diets as boys were, but one-third of boys today are trying to lose weight. (Overall, the percentage of teens who described themselves as overweight between 1991 and now has remained steady at about one-third, according to the U.S. Centers for Disease Control, but the percentage who are trying to lose weight has gone up slightly, from 41.8 percent to 45.6 percent.) It is not even unusual these days for parents to confide in me that their *preteens* are trying to lose weight. A Magellan Health Services study reported that 8 in 10 fifth-grade girls had been on a diet; in an online *Good Housekeeping* survey, one-third of middle school–age girls said that they have cut back on their eating without telling their mothers.

The Adult Obesity Crisis

The increase in childhood obesity rates does not begin to compare to the increase in adult obesity. In the late 1970s, only 15 percent of parents were labeled obese; today, nearly a third of adults are obese, and more than 6 in 10 American adults are overweight. Despite attention to the obesity crisis in recent years, the popularity of the Atkins and South Beach diets, and new government campaigns, obesity continues to increase among adults. In fact, obesity can properly be labeled an adult epidemic. In August 2006, a new report came out (amusingly called "F as in Fat") indicating that adult obesity had increased in recent years in thirty-one states. Adults lead the way for their children, even when we set examples we never want them to follow. As Michael Males wrote in a 2003 *Youth Today* article, "As baby boomers got fatter fast, our kids got fatter slower…. The problem isn't fat kids aging into fat adults but fat adults raising fat kids in their image."

Ouch. That may be impolitic, but the U.S. Surgeon General's Action Report on Obesity in 2001 recognized as much without saying it as starkly. One of its recommendations was to "educate parents about the need to serve as good role models by practicing healthy eating habits and engaging in regular physical activity in order to instill lifelong health habits in their children."

Schools: Helping or Hurting?

In recent years, school systems have been trying to help children eat better. Greg is complaining that he can no longer get chips or ice cream at school, although he likes that wraps are offered as an alternative to sandwiches. Banning soda machines from schools seems like a good idea to me. But frankly, some of what is being done seems not only silly but counterproductive. In some school systems, children have a bar code on their lunch passes that allows parents to control what their children can buy in the cafeteria. Have people forgotten that children swap food at lunchtime? Some schools now take measurements of their students' body mass index and include the information on quarterly report cards. Do parents really want that to be the school system's role? Many school systems have banned parents from bringing in cupcakes and other sweets for birthday parties. I recently heard about a school where parents had to call the principal to have their birthday treats approved in advance. My hometown school board has just banned bake sales from elementary through high school, and parent groups are up in arms about this loss of easy revenue at school activities. I agreed with the dad at the public hearing who said that high school kids are driving cars, dating, voting, going into the military, and in some cases getting pregnant—yet we can't trust them with a cupcake?

Somehow a weekly cupcake in school hardly begins to explain why 1 in 6 American children is overweight. (And what about the other 5 who aren't?) The fact is that healthy eating and exercise habits begin at home; it seems very unlikely that a child who has learned how to eat well at home through both parental modeling and healthy food choices is going to become overweight because of a bag of chips at lunchtime.

Playing Less

One of the major factors for the increase in overweight children is that despite the seemingly endless opportunities for organized sports, they are simply not getting enough physical exercise— much less than most of us got when we were children. The current *Dietary Guidelines for Americans* recommend that children exercise at least sixty minutes every day and limit television watching and computer games (although, as I will discuss, heavy media consumption does not actually decrease a young person's involvement in physical activity. I will go into television watching and other media consumption in chapter 9 and some of the reasons parents limit outdoor play in chapter 8). Today's children are less likely to be taking daily physical education courses, less likely to ride a bike to school, and less likely to just play outside than their parents were. It surprised me to learn that almost half of high school students have no physical education at their schools; no wonder exercise is down.

You probably remember walking or biking to school. According to the Institute of Medicine, in 1969, 9 in 10 children who lived less than 1 mile from school walked or rode a bicycle to school. Ninety percent. Thirty years later, only 1 in 5 children walked and only 1 in 20 rode a bicycle to school. That is a huge decline, and as we will see in chapter 8, this dramatic change is likely born out of parents' overblown fears for their children's safety from child predators. Even more dramatic has been a decline in the amount of time children spend playing outdoors; the average child spends only *eighteen minutes a week* (that's right, a week) playing outside. Fewer than 1 in 10 children (8 percent) play outside each day.

Our misplaced fears and desire to manage our children are limiting children's physical activities in other ways. Several school systems from Massachusetts to South Carolina to Washington State have banned "tag" from their playgrounds, as well as touch football and dodgeball. School administrators say it's because children might get hurt playing these games, but one said on a radio report that it was to protect children's self-esteem. After all, the child who is always left as "it" might get his or her feelings hurt. Come on. Are our children so fragile that we have to protect them from childhood games? (I write this as the girl who was always picked last for teams in elementary school. Yes, it hurt, but I learned to compensate in other ways.)

You *Can* Be Too Thin

It's ironic that even as the number of young people who are overweight begins to climb, some are striving to be thinner and thinner. It's not at all unusual for girls in the youth groups I meet with to complain that they are too fat or that their hips (or other body parts) are too large, even though to me they look lovely. I've over-heard girls in clothing stores say emphatically to each other that they will not buy a certain pair of pants or top because it would mean buying a size 6. The percentage of students who describe themselves as slightly or very overweight has not changed since 1991; about 1 in 3 adolescents has described themselves this way since 1991, although according to U.S. government data, only half that number are considered to be so by medical professionals.

Some young people are turning to extreme measures to lose weight, often unsuccessfully. More than 1 in 10 teens admit having fasted for more than a day to lose weight; 6 percent had taken diet pills or powders without a doctor's advice; and 1 in 20 had vomited or taken laxatives to lose weight. Vomiting or laxative use is nearly three times higher among girls compared to boys. Although it is not negligible in boys, it isn't any higher than it was in 1991: about 4.5 percent. Extreme dieting behavior begins early for some children: 4 percent of sixth graders, 6.5 percent of seventh graders, and 10.5 per-cent of eighth graders admit that they have taken diet pills, powders, or liquids without a doctor's advice (or probably a parent's aware-ness).

Anorexia and *bulimia* were not words I knew growing up, but I did know girls who practiced them. I never vomited or binged and purged, but I do remember that in my early years of high school, I was often on a diet of grapefruits and Tab diet cola. I also recall that one of my close girlfriends in high school regularly used laxatives without her parents' knowledge before a big dance or date. Jane Fonda, in her memoir, *My Life So Far*, describes her twenty-year addiction to bingeing and purging and tells readers that drastic measures for weight control go back to ancient Rome. Anorexia and bulimia are not new conditions.

It may surprise you that despite the fascination our culture holds for very thin celebrities, the number of young people suffering from eating disorders is actually very low, with only 3 out of 1000 young females having anorexia and 1 in 100 having bulimia and binge-eating disorders; boys have one-quarter the rate of anorexia and one-tenth the rate of bulimia of girls. The incidence of eating disorders, particularly anorexia and particularly among fifteen- to twenty-four-year-old girls, increased significantly from the 1930s to the 1970s, but has probably been leveling off since. In other words, despite all the media attention, this is not a new problem and it's not the result of today's super-thin models.

But eating disorders are *very* serious when they do occur. According to the National Association of Anorexia Nervosa and Associated Disorders, 86 percent of all people with eating disorders report the onset of the illness before the age of twenty, with 10 percent reporting its start at the shocking age of ten or younger. Only half the people with eating disorders are ever cured of them. As many as 6 percent will die from them. In fact, it has the highest mortality rate of any mental illness. I remember vividly one woman talking with me about how agonized she felt, begging her teenage daughter to drink even a few drops of water before she was finally hospitalized. In many cases, hospitalization is the only answer.

A recent article in *Newsweek* reports that the age of the youngest anorexic patients at treatment facilities has declined to as young as eight. Although conventional wisdom understood that anorexia is a disease related to cultural images of beauty and demands for perfection among young women, scientists now believe that it is likely to be a genetic disorder that has more to do with brain chemistry than culture. Cynthia Bulike, the director of the eating disorder program at the University of North Carolina, told *Newsweek*, "The environment pulls the trigger, but it is a child's latent vulnerabilities that load the gun." In other words, many young people are affected by the media images of thinness and high-pressure environments, but only a tiny percent go on to have a diagnosable eating disorder.

Parents influence their children's obesity and eating disorders by their own behaviors, but in severe cases genetics are probably a more important influence. For example, a child's birth weight and weight gain in the first year of life are the most telling indicators of who will be overweight in later childhood. But the question remains why all children with a genetic predisposition do not become overweight or develop an eating disorder.

WHAT AFFIRMING PARENTS CAN DO

It's not going to surprise you that parenting style does make a difference in childhood weight issues. In a study published in *Pediatrics* in June 2006, researchers found that Authoritarian mothers were four times more likely than Affirming moms to have children who are overweight by the first grade. Permissive moms were twice as likely as Affirming moms. The lead researcher, Dr. Kyung Rhee, speculated that what we are calling Affirming Parents may help their children make good decisions about food and exercise, and that overly strict parents may be causing their children to turn to food for comfort. In an interview about the article, she suggested that parents set rules for eating, such as you must eat one vegetable at each meal, but that children should get to pick which vegetable and how much they want to eat.

So, what should you do if you're concerned about your child eating either too much or too little? Experts strongly recommend that parents never put an overweight child on a diet without medical input and advice. In many cases, overweight children will simply "grow into" their weight as they go through puberty. It's just not true that an overweight child will always grow into an overweight teenager without being put on a diet. I find it important to remind parents of chubby preadolescent children that during the preteen years it is important for children to be gaining weight. During the transition to adolescence, bones are thickening, hearts and brains are getting larger, muscles are being built, and weight gain is not only expected but required. In addition, dieting may actually trigger reactions in the brain that can begin eating disorders.

Dr. Craig Johnson, director of an eating disorders program in Tulsa, Oklahoma, advised *Newsweek* readers, "If you have anorexia in the family and your 11-year-old tells you she is about to go on a diet and is thinking about joining the track team, you want to be very careful about how you approach her request." She needs support for healthy eating and moderate exercise, not diets and daily three-hour workouts.

It is easier to teach our children healthy attitudes and behaviors about food early in their lives because it gets much more difficult to do so once patterns are set. But as your child moves into later stages of adolescence, in this area as in others, you want to think "advisory committee," not "board of directors." Several parents have come to me lately with concerns about their teenage daughters who have put on a lot of weight. In one case, a mom removed food from her daughter's plate; in another, the parents worried that despite taking their daughter to a nutrition counselor and monitoring her food intake at meals, she continued to gain weight; in another case, a fifteen-year-old girl has to ask her mother before she can have a can of soda. All the parents want their daughters to lose weight. And all the daughters manage somehow to eat enough food when their folks are not around to continue to gain. The reality is that no one can be forced to lose weight if he or she is not motivated to do so. Many women know that they can't get their husbands to lose weight until they are ready to do so, no matter how much the wives talk about it or fix low-calorie meals; the same is true for their adolescents. Letting them own the solution to their weight is much more effective. And of course, as in other areas, it's important to seek medical and psychological evaluations if warranted. Here's what we can do:

1. Model healthy eating and exercising habits.

There are many recommendations for preventing obesity and eating disorders in young people, and the recommendations for both ends of the spectrum are similar. They include healthy body image, healthy eating, and physical exercise in your family for *all* members of the family. In general, they emphasize role modeling in the family and examining our own thoughts, attitudes, and behaviors about body size, weight, attractiveness, and self-image. In other words, the most important things parents can do are to eat well ourselves, to engage in regular moderate exercise, and to create an environment in which our children can do the same. By modeling healthy attitudes toward food and weight, we help raise fit children, and we can also do something about our own weight problems. After all, it is adults who are driving their children to the fast food places (although, as you will see in the discussion about viral marketing, the fast food companies themselves are doing everything they can to get your children to pester you to bring them there).

Experts in both obesity and eating disorders encourage that food never be used as a comfort, a reward, or a punishment. Requiring children to clean their plate when they are not hungry is Authoritarian behavior that can backfire; double desserts for a good grade on yesterday's quiz from a Permissive parent are likely to as well. We want to teach our children that eating is primarily about nutrition, not emotional fulfillment.

2. Don't make negative comments about your own weight.

We also need to guard against making negative comments about our own bodies and weight to our children, and to examine what the National Eating Disorders Association calls *weightism*. According to Dr. Michael Levine of the National Eating Disorders Association, it's important that we "help children appreciate and resist the ways in which television, magazines, and other media distort the true diversity of human body types and imply that a slender body means power, excitement, popularity, or perfection."

3. Educate your children about the power of advertising.

Reports on addressing childhood and adolescent obesity generally suggest limiting how much television children are allowed to watch. According to a review by the Kaiser Family Foundation, the "majority of scientific research indicates that children who spend the most time with media are more likely to be overweight." The presumption has been that children are watching more television than we did, and that is causing them to exercise less. It turns out that children who watch a lot of television do not get less physical exercise than other children, and the average number of hours a child watches television a week has actually gone down almost an hour a day since 1981.

Rather, researchers now think it is children's exposure through media to food advertising and marketing that may be behind the correlation. The typical child sees forty thousand ads a year on television, and the vast majority of ads on children's TV are for candy, cereal, soda, and fast foods. I saw a *Dateline* segment recently in which even two-year-olds could identify the McDonald's Golden

Arches logo. Many popular children's television characters have been morphed into food products. In my local supermarket I found Sponge Bob macaroni and cheese, Pirates of the Caribbean cereal, and Dora the Explorer fruit-flavor snacks. (According to a story on National Public Radio, if you bought all of the Dora products, you would spend over $3,000!) Such advertising and use of characters is, in the words of the advertising industry, designed to increase "pester power"—children demanding that their parents buy products that they have seen advertised on television.

In 1750 B.C., the Code of Hammurabi made it a crime punishable by death to sell anything to a child without first obtaining a power of attorney. Not so today. If television advertising was a big concern in the 1980s and 1990s, parents have an additional concern today: the use of advertising online targeted to your children. The Kaiser Family Foundation, in a 2006 study, found that seventy-seven brands are marketing directly to your children on the Web. Their sites are visited by over 12 million children between the ages of two to eleven each month. Three-quarters of these sites use their products or characters for online games, like Chips Ahoy Soccer Shoot Out, the M&M's Trivia Game, and a childhood online Coca-Cola room.

Two-thirds of the sites use viral marketing techniques—that means they provide your children with e-cards or e-coupons to send to their friends, in some cases promising your child extra points or more coupons for sending them out to multiple children. One in four of these sites has a child membership, and in half of them your child can sign up without your permission. Yet another reason, as I will discuss in a later chapter, to monitor your child's Internet use. No wonder our children ask for foods and fast food outlets by brand name!

4. Talk with your children about healthy eating.

Our best defense is using Affirming Parenting techniques. Talk with your children about healthy eating. Teach them to read labels to assess whether a product is healthy. Help them understand that just because a product is labeled "healthy" or "low fat" does not mean that it is. Talk with them about why food companies use popular cartoon characters to help sell their food. Help them critique commercials. Be sure you know what Internet sites your child is visiting. Try to eliminate the trips to McDonald's and Burger King, or at least make them no more than a weekly treat. Many parents have told me that they give in on junk food because it's easier than making their child unhappy. Affirming Parents know it's worth making their children temporarily unhappy if it means helping them learn good nutrition habits.

5. Make family dinners part of your routine.

One of the most important tools for both healthy eating and creating a sense of parent-child connectedness is the family dinner. Regular family dinners may be the best way to curb obesity and keep a vulnerable child from an eating disorder. Serving healthy foods in a pleasant atmosphere while allowing your child and teen the right to decide what and how much to eat reinforces your Affirming Parent approach.

In a study of how American children spend their time, sociologist Sandra Hofferth found that the amount of time a family spent together at meals was the best predictor of children's higher academic scores and fewer behavioral problems. Family dinners were a stronger influence than church, sports, studying, school, and other activities as a predictor. The National Adolescent Health study found that teens who have dinner five or more times a week with a parent had higher academic success, fewer behavioral problems, and lower rates of alcohol and drug use and suicide risk, and began having sexual intercourse later.

Eight in ten parents believe that family dinners are important, and in at least 60 percent of homes, families eat together at least five nights a week. In a 2006 CBS/*New York Times* poll, every family said that they ate dinner together on average five nights a week. In 1979, when we were teens and children, the average was three nights a week. The amount of time spent in family meals has declined by more than one hour since 1981, however, from nine hours a week to seven and a half hours a week.

Depending on the study, though, a minority of teens—a quarter to a third—say that they rarely eat dinner with their families or do so only a couple of nights a week. Many parents have shared with me that they are either too tired to cook or that their family members just have too many different schedules to coordinate dinner together. Clearly, making the effort to have regular family meals is important, and there is nothing wrong with takeout, salads, or sandwiches. In an essay, my son recently wrote that he was forced to learn to cook because he was tired of Lean Cuisine frozen dinners and pizza.

The point is to sit down together on a regular basis and talk. Turning off the TV during dinner is a no-brainer for improving family communication; but the Kaiser Family Foundation reports that a whopping 63 percent of families report that the TV is on during meals. Setting dinner at a regular time is helpful; it is more likely with low-income than higher-income families. Using manners and talking together make a difference. Having a no-iPod, cell-phones-off, no-television rule means that family conversations can occur.

Family dinners offer an opportunity to instill a sense of gratitude and spirituality in your home. Many families offer short blessings or prayers before meals. In our home, we start our meals with a simple moment of grace followed by each of us saying what we are thankful for that day. Another friend's family routinely shares the hardest thing each faced that day.

Family dinners also provide you with an opportunity to talk to your children and find out what's going on with them. In too many children's lives, there is little family communication: only 1 in 4 children ages six to twelve reports that the family engages in household conversations during the week, and in those the conversations averaged thirty minutes—just four minutes a day! Taking the time to talk about what each person did during the day is an easy way to begin dinnertime discussions. Discussing current events as a family shows your children that you respect them and their thoughts.

The biggest problem that I hear about family dinners is that families and children are too busy to plan them, too busy to cook them, and too busy to eat them. Parents tell me that they stop at fast food restaurants between sports and music lessons, and that everyone in their family is on a different schedule. In the next chapter, we'll look at how overstressed and overscheduled this generation of children really is and what is happening because of it.

TEST YOUR FEAR FACTOR

1. Compared to 1981, children today have:
   a. More free time.
   b. Less free time.
   c. About the same amount of free time.

2. Compared to 1981, children today are involved in:
   a. More activities each week.
   b. Fewer activities each week.
   c. About the same number of activities each week.

3. Involvement in many extracurricular activities:
   a. Is hurting our children.
   b. Has positive effects.
   c. Has little effect either way.

4. Graduates of Ivy League colleges, as compared to graduates of state schools, are:
   a. More likely to have higher incomes.
   b. Less likely to have higher incomes.
   c. Likely to have similar incomes.

5. Most young people:
   a. Are unhappy with their lives.
   b. Are happy with their lives.
   c. Wish their lives were different.

* * * * *
Answers: 1. c; 2. b; 3. b; 4. c; 5. b.

CHAPTER 4

The Myth of the Overscheduled, Overstressed Generation

WE HAVE ALL HEARD about how overscheduled and overstressed our children and teens are. My colleague Rabbi Bob Orkand told me a story about needing to schedule additional time with a twelve-year-old who was having trouble with the Torah portion of his bar mitzvah preparations. The boy told the rabbi that he was too busy to meet with him outside of class. Bob persevered, telling him that this was important. At that point, the twelve-year-old reached into his backpack, took out his Palm Pilot, and began searching its date-book for an opening. (You have to wonder if at the end of every day, each member of his family syncs their PDA to a central computer so they can coordinate their calendars together.)

There is no doubt that most of us, including our children, are leading busy and full lives. But the media portrays children and teenagers as overscheduled, overstressed, and overparented—in other words, a mess. Parents are portrayed as overinvolved "helicopter parents" or underinvolved with their late elementary school–through high school–age child. How do these issues play out in our real lives?

FACT vs. FEAR

Despite the media stories and our concerns about how stressed our children and teens are, most studies report that young people feel good about themselves, good about their parents, and happy

• 63

about their lives. Seven in ten teens, for example, report that they have a positive view of their personal future and a positive view of their families. Half of teenagers say "I am usually happy."

And, though their parents might be portrayed as either overbearing or underinvolved, young people today generally like their parents. A 2000 poll of 84,000 young people in grades 6 to 12 found that 80 percent would go to one or both of their parents with a serious problem; 84 percent said that their parents have told them they loved them in recent days; and 78 percent had recently told their parents that they loved them. More than 9 in 10 said that their parents are either always or generally supportive, and 86 percent would grade their parents an A or B in parenting.

It is important to point out that this concern about overstressed and overscheduled children is not new. Dr. David Elkind wrote a book way back in 1981 called *The Hurried Child: Growing Up Too Fast Too Soon*. He may have been writing about you. Andree Brooks in 1989 wrote a book titled *Children of Fast Track Parents* that described how achievement-oriented parents were putting too many pressures to achieve on their children. Today, articles abound on how busy our children are and how many young people are being raced from a lesson to a sports event to a place-of-worship event to a volunteer event, and so on. The implication is that parents are forcing their children into these activities, and that compared to our own childhood, children today are overscheduled and overstressed because of it. Guess what? Not true.

ONLY SO MANY HOURS

Because of the pioneering work of Dr. Sandra Hofferth, we have a pretty good idea of how children aged six to twelve have been spending their time over the past two and a half decades. Dr. Hofferth began studying children's use of time while she was at the University of Michigan; today she is a professor in the Department of Family Studies at the University of Maryland, College Park.

The bulk of a child's week is taken up by required activities such as sleeping, eating, going to school, and personal care. Elementary school children spend most of their time each week sleeping (just over 69 hours in 2003, actually up from 65½ hours in 1981, and comparable to adults' average of 70 hours), in school (33½ hours in 2003, up from 29 hours in 1981), eating (7½ hours a week, down 1 hour from 1981), and doing personal care (almost 8 hours per week in 2003, up from 6½ hours in 1981). After sleeping and school, the most frequent activity is television watching (13½ hours a week), which has dropped dramatically from the 20 hours you may have spent watching TV in 1981. Before you bemoan children's 13 hours a week in front of a television set, consider that adults on average actually spend 19 hours a week watching TV.

Children's free time for other activities *has* gone down, but only a tiny 4 percent since 1997. On average today, children ages six to twelve have almost 7 hours a day of "discretionary" time; take away a few minutes, and that's not much different than it was twenty years ago. That tiny percent change is because children are sleeping more and the school day is now longer, not because they are in more organized activities. In fact, despite all the media stories on children being so much busier today, according to these intensive research studies, children actually on average do five fewer activities per day on weekdays and one fewer activity on a weekend than children did in 1981.

But there are some differences in how children are spending their free time compared to twenty or thirty years ago. Children today are more likely to spend time studying, doing art activities, and participating in youth groups than we were. They are less likely to be spending time at a faith-based institution. They are playing a little under nine hours a week, but that's almost an hour and a half more than nine- to twelve-year-olds played in 1981. Only five minutes are spent on average each week on hobbies, and only one and a half hours are spent reading.

GOOD NEWS

Contrary to media warnings about the "overscheduled child," the research shows that involvement in a diverse array of activities may actually be beneficial to children and teens. *How* children spend their time makes a difference in certain outcomes in their lives, but not as many as you might have guessed. For example, not surprisingly, spending more time reading leads to higher achievement scores. But the amount of time a child spends watching television, studying, playing, creating art, or doing hobbies was not associated with either external behavioral problems, like acting out at school, or internal behavioral issues, like anxiety or depression. In a review of the literature, the nonprofit organization Child Trends found that after-school activities help children develop social skills, improve their relationships with peers and adults, and improve their academic scores. They lead to higher self-esteem, lower alcohol and substance use, and higher social competency. And they help parents with child care, which 7 in 10 working parents say they need.

The Search Institute, another nonprofit research institution specializing in children and youth, has found that "healthy, caring, and responsible" teens are actively involved in a variety of school, community, and religious institutions. In their research studies of more than 350,000 young people, they found that high-functioning youth were involved in more than seventeen hours a week of activities, in addition to the time they spend in school. These teens spent, on average, three hours a week in creative activities, three hours in youth programs, and one or more hours at a faith-based institution, and they read for pleasure three or more hours a week. And young people seem to be choosing their own activities; in a study by Columbia University professor Suniya Luthar, 9 in 10 young people in grades 6 through 12 say that a parent has never made them do something against their desires, such as take a music lesson, play a sport, or join a club.

As I briefly discussed in the last chapter, many children are spending more time in organized sports, perhaps because parents recognize that this may be the only way their children get physical exercise. But it may surprise you to know that the number of hours children spend in organized sports peaked a decade ago and has been declining since. In 2002, it had dropped back to levels similar to what it was in 1981.

For women, there has been a dramatic change since I was a child in the 1960s, when only the most athletically talented girls played organized sports. Title IX, passed in 1975, made a difference in opening sports up to girls, and that is reflected in the 1981 numbers. The number of girls playing on teams has increased significantly since the 1970s. In today's high schools, there are likely to be girls' hockey teams, lacrosse teams, and soccer teams.

The good news is that organized sports provide an opportunity for almost all children and teens to engage in physical activity. We are not just "soccer moms," but basketball, baseball, T-ball, gymnastics, and football moms and dads. Nationally, more than half of high school students (56 percent) play on one or more sports teams, with 60 percent of the boys and 50 percent of the girls having been on a team. The proportion of children on sports teams is even higher for younger kids; 60 percent of children ages six to twelve participate in organized sports, significantly higher than when we were children, although not as high as it was at its peak, in 1997.

Some parents have confided in me that they are worried that their children and teens are spending too much time in organized sports when they should just be hanging out or playing. Although this is an understandable concern, it turns out that as long as there is moderation and not too much stress from parents who emphasize winning at all costs, participation in sports is good for most young people. In fact, rather than being problematic, spending more time on sports is correlated with lower behavioral problems and higher academic scores. For most young people, the more active they are, the better.

But organized sports for young people have gotten a bad rap. News stories abounded in the late 90s and early 2000s about over-involved sports parents, and the term *soccer mom* entered our vocabulary. Perhaps you remember the 2001 news story about the Massachusetts parent, Thomas Junta, who killed his ten-year-old son's hockey coach, Michael Costin, because, ironically, he felt that Costin had been too rough on his son. That was an extreme situation and outcome, yet most of us can recount stories of parents' bad behavior on the sidelines. Some town leagues have actually passed "good sportsmanship" policies for the *parents* of the players. I have certainly seen parents yelling at their children for less than optimal performance on the soccer field, although I more often see parents hugging their children and consoling them after missed goals.

21st-CENTURY CHALLENGES

Despite all this good news, there are some real challenges in today's world that can have a deleterious effect on our children's lives. To start, despite their involvement in sports, children today spend much less time playing outdoors than we did. In 2003, *only 1 in 10 children played outside during an average week.* The amount of time children spend playing outdoors has been steadily declining since 1981 (but it was only forty-six minutes on average a week for nine- to twelve-year-olds even then), and has gone down eighteen minutes in just the last decade. It doesn't just seem that our children play outside less than we did; they do play outside less. I'll talk more in chapter 8 about how our misguided fears about our children's safety are keeping them indoors unnecessarily and causing what author and child advocate Richard Louv aptly named "nature-deficit disorder."

Overstressed Parents, Overstressed Children

Perhaps part of our concern about our children and teens being overscheduled and overstressed stems from the fact that we feel so overstressed and overscheduled ourselves. The lines between work and home have certainly blurred for many of us with the advent of e-mail, BlackBerries, personal organizers, and computers in our homes. At an evening program I led recently at a private school, two women in the front row used their BlackBerries during almost my entire presentation. I now ask audiences to turn off their cell phones *and* their BlackBerries. How much stress is in your own life? And are you stressed about your child's achievements?

Overemphasis on Children's Achievements

The greater emphasis placed on children's achievements compared to previous generations can go a long way toward explaining the way children and teens are spending their time. The emphasis on children's achievements at school, as exemplified by the No Child Left Behind Act, may be responsible for the longer school day, as well as more homework. When my son was in the sixth and seventh grades, on some nights he had two to three hours of homework.

In 2000, Dr. Alvin Rosenfeld, a child psychiatrist, co-wrote a book titled *The Over-Scheduled Child: Avoiding the Hyper-parenting Trap*. I tend to agree with his statement that "parenting has become the most competitive sport in America." He writes that today's parents become "over-involved in every detail of their children's academic, athletic, and social lives. They over-enrich their children's environment and over-schedule them." School officials complain about our generation of "helicopter parents" who are always right there; one dean of a college told me that in the last few years, his colleagues have renamed them "hovercraft parents," ever present in their soon-to-be-adult children's lives. I know several parents whose college students e-mail them their papers for editing. An article in September 2006 in the *Boston Globe* included interviews from college deans asking parents of freshmen to try backing off a bit and encouraging their children to solve their own problems. Such overinvolvement and the stress for success placed on our children begins way before college. It's good that we're involved in our children's lives, but hovering can hurt our children and teenagers in surprising ways.

For example, in a study of affluent suburban teens, young people who perceived their parents as applying achievement pressures were much more likely to use alcohol and other drugs. Pressures to succeed at school are significant predictors of substance abuse. (I'll talk more about alcohol and drug use in chapter 7.) Ironically, such pressures do not lead to an increase in academic success as measured by grades or test scores, and often result in greater internal distress and substance abuse, especially in girls. The study, by Dr. Suniya Luthar of Columbia University, found that suburban girls who set excessively high personal standards for themselves experience greater individual distress and external behavioral problems. It is true, as psychologist Alice Miller wrote in her wonderful book *The Drama of the Gifted Child*, that when children believe their parents value them more for being competent than for who they are, they begin to rely on their accomplishments for their sense of self-worth. Adults, too: the more we focus on external accomplishments, such as money and material acquisitions, rather than personal internal goals, like self-knowledge and good relationships, the more at risk we are for mental illness.

This overemphasis on achievement spills over into organized sports, as well. As I've mentioned, sports have lots to offer: they provide an opportunity for your child to exercise, develop team spirit, learn cooperation skills, and feel part of a larger group. But some parents go too far, forcing their children into a single sport at a young age, dreaming of high school championships and athletic scholarships, rather than allowing their children to try many different activities and even play at ones that they aren't particularly good at. And some parents place too much emphasis on winning and skill development as opposed to having fun; sports then become one more way to overstress and overschedule your child. Your attitude and approach make the difference.

Focusing on organized sports may have an additional downside: it may actually be keeping our children from learning to play with other children on their own. A friend of mine told me this story. Her ten-year-old daughter stayed after school for softball practice. The whole team was there, the equipment was available, but the coach did not show up. Now, if that had happened to us as children, we probably would have divided into teams and played anyway. Not today. The children simply sat down and waited until it was time for their parents to pick them up. When my friend asked her daughter, "How come you didn't play a game?" her daughter answered casually and with disdain, "Mom, there was no one there to organize us." Our children would benefit if we gave them more opportunities to "just play" with other children without adult involvement. Perhaps the recent reduction in time spent in organized sports indicates that parents in the past seven to ten years have begun to realize this. One can hope.

The College Admissions Stress Test

Nowhere does parents' overemphasis on their children's success play out more than in the competitive race of the college admissions process. Getting their children into the right college seems to be an obsession of parents from the middle and upper class, especially those of us on the East or West coasts. My friends who live in the square states in the middle of the country seem more immune. Their children are often content to plan on attending the state schools, which offer an excellent education at a more modest cost.

Not so for many of us in places like Fairfield County, Connecticut, or Marin County, California. According to a March 21, 2006, article in the *New York Times*, high school seniors interested in the most selective universities now apply to ten to twelve schools. One guidance counselor told of a student who applied to twenty-eight schools, but many knew students who had applied to more than twenty. Compare that to the three, four, or five that you probably applied to (I remember the mantra: one safety, one or two you liked but were not sure, one stretch.) According to the article, the main reasons for this "frenzy" are "growing anxiety about admissions, stoked by college ranking guides, the news media, and often parents. Some students are desperate to do anything to get into a brand-name institution—including applying to many of them."

Here's how a high school senior in my Connecticut town put it in our local paper: "One of the biggest stressors today is getting into college. But you cannot just have good grades anymore; you have to be almost perfect. Not only that, but colleges expect us to handle all of this stuff. They want us to volunteer, take AP courses, play sports, and get into their schools." She plaintively asks, "But do they know the level of stress that we go through and how much we have on our plates?"

Is placing this stress on your child worth it? Probably not. As a recent *Time* magazine cover story, "Who Needs Harvard?" put it, there are hundreds of good colleges for young people. A college admissions officer is quoted explaining that "college is a match to be made, not a prize to be won." The article reminds parents that studies show that at least 70 percent of students get into their first-choice school. They also cite a 2002 *Quarterly Journal of Economics* study "showing that students who were accepted at top schools but for various reasons went to less selective ones were earning just as much 20 years later as their peers from more highly selective colleges."

WHAT AFFIRMING PARENTS CAN DO

In addition to attending to the stress in our own lives, there are many things Affirming Parents can do to help ensure that our children are not overscheduled and overstressed.

1. Emphasize learning goals, not performance goals.

It should come as no surprise that children of Affirming Parents often do the best in school. Two researchers from the Institute for the Academic Advancement of Youth at the Johns Hopkins University did a study of parents' achievement goals and perfectionism in their academically talented children. They differentiated parents who emphasize learning goals ("Do your best," "Learn as much as you can from this course") and performance-goal parents ("Make sure you get an A in all your classes"). They found that the children of performance-goal parents reported a greater concern about making mistakes, were more likely to have what they call "dysfunctional perfectionism," and were more likely to doubt themselves.

Conversely, children of learning-goal parents actually performed better in their classes. Counter to popular opinion, the majority of the parents of these academically talented young people were "learning-goal" parents: their primary emphasis was on having their children understand the class material and demonstrate intellectual growth. Parents who had perfectionist tendencies themselves were most likely to adopt performance rather than learning goals for their children, thus passing on their own dysfunctional style of dealing with mistakes. The Johns Hopkins researchers conclude, "Parents who encourage independence but clearly set standards for their children, that have an authoritative [affirming] style are more likely to have children who excel in school. These parents may be sensitive to individual needs and adhere to socially acceptable rules, therefore having both learning and performance goals for their children." Being Affirming, not Authoritarian, once again helps our children achieve the goals we have for them. Not surprisingly, Permissive Parents who believe that school is their children's business and generally stay uninvolved usually have children who do less well academically.

Stop and think for a moment: What messages about school success are you giving your children? Grades and scores, or learning for learning's sake? What would your children say?

2. Know your own child.

Some children need encouragement to do much of anything outside of school; some children need to be encouraged to cut back.

In our home, we have set a guideline of two organized activities a week outside of school and church; one of our children needed to be encouraged to reach that goal; the other needed our help keeping it to that. You know your child best. Guide him or her in choosing extracurricular activities.

3. Give your children downtime.

They need time to write, play, think, daydream, fantasize, and be creative. They need time, in Greg's words, "to just buzz out." Allowing your child to feel and deal with boredom is a good thing. It is okay for kids to do nothing. I have always asked my children not to use the expression "I'm bored." I point out that they have the ability to create activities for themselves, or simply to sit, listen to music, and daydream.

I also think it is good for children and teens to spend downtime with their parents, just relaxing, vegging out, being together. We do not always have to plan family activities. Sometimes it's good for everyone, children and parents alike, to just hang out in the living room doing nothing together. Or reading, playing games, or talking.

Some communities are trying to help families have more of that downtime. Since 2003, for example, the town of Ridgewood, New Jersey, has held an annual Family Night, when every organization in town agrees to go "dark" and not have a scheduled activity. Surely one such evening a year is not enough downtime to spend with our kids. In my community, the clergy are working with school and sports officials to make Sunday morning a game- and practice-free zone. We were losing too many of our middle school and high school kids to sport and play practices on Saturday or Sunday mornings, when the clergy would like them to be in church or synagogue for religious education.

4. Be a good "sport."

Sports are good for your children—if they enjoy the sport! Teach them that winning is not the primary focus of being on a sports team. More important, sports can teach children teamwork, get them needed physical activity, and offer them a sense of belonging. Parents should support their child's involvement in activities that children (not parents) choose, be happy for their children's successes and supportive of their losses, and not criticize or try to improve their children's performances. Leave that to the coaches.

5. Let your child choose the college.

Parents need to lighten up on the college admissions front and let their children largely be in charge of the application process. I have known too many parents who have pushed their children to go to a school of the parents' choosing, and then—either by failing, getting involved with drugs or alcohol, developing an eating disorder, or another form of acting-out during freshman year—the teenager lets the parents know that they chose the wrong place. If you can, try to resist even beginning this discussion with your children until their junior year of high school. Enjoy the process of visiting schools with your children, but let them decide which schools they might want to attend. Let them know that there is a right school for everyone, and resist the temptation to see the college application process as your process. Alyssa grew weary of adults asking her, "Where are you applying?" during her senior year in high school; I was weary of this being a major topic of conversation with the adults in my life as well.

6. Stay involved, stay connected, and set limits.

Despite all the reports of overinvolvement by parents, the irony is that too many parents are underinvolved, both logistically and emotionally. Many of us are working when our preteens and teens come home from school, and we need to find ways both to stay connected emotionally and to assure their safety. One-quarter of sixth graders, one-quarter of seventh-grade girls, and almost half of seventh-grade boys report that no adults supervise them after school. No supervision correlates with young people being more likely to be distressed, more likely to engage in delinquent behavior, and more likely to abuse alcohol and other substances. It makes sense: if we're not home to monitor our tweens, they're more likely to get into trouble. Once again, we need to seek a way to balance our children's need for independence with their need for us to be involved in their lives.

I have had the good fortune of working in a home office for the past seven years, but if I am out of town giving lectures or working with congregations, Gregory knows to call both me and his dad on our cell phones when he gets home from school for a quick check-in. Unless I'm in the middle of a speech or radio interview, I always take that 3:20 p.m. call. He is not allowed to bring friends over when we're not home, and he has a daily list of chores plus homework that are to be completed before he can watch television. He knows the consequence if we were to find out that his homework was not completed: we would sit down every night to go over his homework with him in great depth until the next marking period. You may set other limits, but the point is to set them and to let your tween or teen children know that you care what they do after school, whether you are there or not.

It is our responsibility as parents to help set the limits for our children both for outside activities and in our homes. We need to stay connected and involved enough to know when our children might be feeling overwhelmed, under pressure, or simply stressed-out. But we also need to remind ourselves that sometimes it's pressure from parents that is causing our children and teens to feel over-stressed.

The goal for most Affirming Parents is to raise children and teens who feel happy with themselves and who are satisfied with their lives. Unfortunately, many of today's children and youth struggle with learning disabilities, depression, and other mental health problems. These are not new problems; some of us struggled with these same issues when we were children. What's new are better screening and diagnosis, new understanding of how we learn and how the brain develops, and newer and better medications. The good news is that we know more than our parents did about how to help our children cope with these problems.

TEST YOUR FEAR FACTOR

1. The proportion of children and teenagers facing mental health issues is:
   a. 1 in 2.
   b. 1 in 4.
   c. 1 in 5.

2. The proportion of teenagers experiencing signs of depression today, as compared to 1999, is:
   a. More.
   b. Less.
   c. The same.

3. The percentage of teenagers who have seriously considered suicide today, as compared to fifteen years ago, is:
   a. Higher.
   b. Lower.
   c. The same.

4. The use of mood-regulating prescription medications by children and adolescents is:
   a. Increasing.
   b. Decreasing.
   c. Staying the same.

* * * * *

Answers: 1. c; 2. c; 3. b; 4. a.

CHAPTER 5

Knowing Their Minds: Raising Emotionally Healthy Children

EXPERTS *AND* PARENTS have always known that people between the ages of ten and twenty think and feel differently than younger children and adults. In the mid-twentieth century, psychologist Jean Piaget wrote that young children are concrete thinkers, and they develop into abstract thinkers in their later adolescent years. In 1916, in a seminal book called *Adolescence*, G. Stanley Hall wrote about the *sturm und drang* ("storm and stress") of adolescence to explain the emotional peaks and valleys that many young people go through. Every parent of a thirteen-year-old knows that young people can swing from mature and thoughtful to belligerent and impulsive in a matter of minutes.

Young people today are no different in this respect than we were as children and teens. But the field of neuroscience—the study of the biology of the brain—now allows us to understand why young people think and act the way they do. According to a report published by the National Campaign to Prevent Teenage Pregnancy titled "The Adolescent Brain: A Work in Progress": "Contrary to long-held ideas that the brain was mostly grown up—fully cooked—by the end of childhood, it is now clear that adolescence is a time of profound brain growth and change. In fact, the brain of an early adolescent in comparison to that of a late adolescent differs measurably in anatomy, biochemistry, and physiology."

Using magnetic resonance imaging (MRI), scientists are now studying how young people process information and how their brains change during the preteen and teen years. In brief, here are some of their discoveries:

- The prefrontal cortex, which helps set priorities, organize ideas, and control impulses, is one of the last parts of the brain to mature. The prefrontal cortex helps us understand the difference between appropriate and inappropriate behavior, adjust our behavior as the situation changes, make plans for the future, experience empathy, and have insights into ourselves and others. It will not surprise most parents of eight- to fifteen-year-olds to learn that this part of their brains is still under construction.

- The parts of the brain seem to communicate better with one another as adulthood approaches, helping us to learn and understand rules, laws, and socially appropriate ways of behaving.

- The "wiring" for good decision making in the brain is being formed throughout adolescence. MRIs show that teens are more likely to react from the amygdala, the portion of the brain that experiences fear, threat, and danger, than from their prefrontal cortex, which is linked to reason and judgment. Adults are more likely to use their intellect to think through decisions; teenagers are more likely to make decisions based on their instincts or feelings. The younger a teen is, the more likely he or she is to yield to impulses without thinking through the consequences.

- Because so much brain development is under way during the teen years, alcohol and other drug use may be especially harmful at this time. Not only can it potentially harm normative brain development, but young people's limited but developing capacity for decision making is further compromised by substance abuse.

What does all this mean? It means that what parents have always known about young people has now been proved biologically: teens and tweens have difficulty making good decisions when situations are complex, they have difficulty controlling their impulses, and they have difficulty planning ahead effectively. In the early years of adolescence, in particular, they often do not have the neurological ability to think through the consequences of their actions. This new information from neuroscience can help us understand why younger teens are less likely to use contraception when they have sex or more likely to drink to the point of inebriation if they have access to alcohol.

Although scientists have much more to learn about the brain, current knowledge can help you think through your own parenting style and what you can do to help your child make good decisions about sex, alcohol, and other drugs. The new brain research provides concrete evidence for Affirming Parents: young people need their parents (and other caring adults) to help them learn specific skills and help them set limits on their behavior. It helps explain why the teenage children of Authoritarian and Affirming Parents generally engage in fewer risk-taking behaviors: these parents provide their children with clear boundaries to help them avoid situations that might tempt them to engage in risks, and provide them with clear consequences, so their children know exactly what will happen if they do. The neuroscience of the developing brain supports what we know from the parenting literature about what is likely to be effective in helping your children make healthy choices about alcohol, other drugs, and sex: unconditional love, joint limit setting, and consistent consequences all can make a difference.

We also know much more than professionals and parents did when we were children about how conditions and illnesses can affect our children's and teens' brains and their ability to function well.

LEARNING DISABILITIES AND BEHAVIOR PROBLEMS

Surely we all remember the kids in our classes in elementary school and middle school who never seemed to sit still, who were the class clowns, who seemed smart but never got good grades—the kids who seemed to get yelled at all the time.

Some of them may have been treated twenty or thirty years ago for what was then known as "hyperactive child syndrome." Ritalin was created back in 1957, and was first prescribed for children with behavior problems in the early '60s. Since 1980, children and teens have been diagnosed as having ADD—attention deficit disorder—

or, more recently, ADHD, attention deficit/hyperactivity disorder. ADHD has been a formal diagnosis for only twenty years. Depending on the study, from 2 to 12 percent of children are diagnosed with ADHD, with the incidence being twice as common among boys as girls. It's a neurological disorder affecting at least two million children in the United States, and it can cause problems with school relationships, depression, and substance abuse.

There is considerable debate about whether ADHD is being overdiagnosed or misdiagnosed. Dr. Paul Steinberg and other psychiatrists say that "the term attention deficit disorder turns out to be a misnomer. Most people who have it actually have remarkably good attention spans as long as they are doing activities that they enjoy or find stimulating...essentially ADHD is a problem dealing with the menial work of daily life, the tedium involved in many school situations and 9-to-5 jobs." He says the real issue is that "these children need hands-on learning, field work, computers and games rather than books. Rather than medicating children to conform, perhaps it is time for the schools to finally recognize that children need the school environment to recognize that we learn differently."

Although many experts, including the major children's medical organizations, disagree with him and believe medications are indicated for children who have a definitive diagnosis of ADHD, some research studies do suggest that he is on to something. In one fascinating study published in the *American Journal of Public Health* in 2004, children with ADHD who played outside in environments with trees experienced a significant decrease in their symptoms. According to a news article, these children "were calmer, more focused, and more able to follow directions after a time outside, especially in settings like a park or backyard." Whether they were helped by the exercise or the natural setting was not conclusive, but surely encouraging children with this disorder to get exercise before doing homework is a good idea. Looking at alternative schools that affirm different learning styles may be an effective answer for a child with ADHD, too.

It also helps if they can get up and move in the classroom. According to the ERIC Digest, an online resource for educators, "even a small amount of movement can help discharge energy that is so critical for these students. It is for this reason that a common consequence for not completing homework, i.e., losing recess, is actually counter-productive with overactive children." In a comprehensive study in the late 1990s of 570 children with ADHD, medication plus behavioral and psychological counseling was found to more effective than medication alone.

Although parenting styles do not correlate with whose children have ADHD (this is a neurological disorder, not an environmental one), parent training for children with ADHD sounds very close to the skills of the Affirming Parent. According to the Duke University health Web site, parenting training includes "helping parents maintain consistent rules at home, teaching them how to deliver effective commands, and showing them how to reward desirable behaviors to reinforce them and create consequences for unacceptable behaviors to reduce their recurrence." The American Academy of Pediatrics encourages parents of children with ADHD to set specific goals, provide positive reinforcements and consequences, and to be consistent. These are the hallmarks of Affirming Parenting for any child.

We are also recognizing today that children and teens can experience mental health problems, something that was often dismissed thirty years ago.

MORE THAN THE BLUES

A teenage girl recently said to me, "You know, everyone thinks it's so great to be a teenager today. But I think it sucks. There is so much pressure to be popular, to be athletic, to get good grades. I am exhausted." She reminded me of an eighth-grade girl I worked with many years ago who told me she couldn't wait to grow up because she had not enjoyed her childhood at all. When I ask audiences of parents at middle schools if they remember enjoying their seventh-grade year, only two or three people raise their hands. And then I quip to the audience, "Those are the people who made the rest of us miserable." People nod in agreement.

But aren't preteens and teenagers supposed to be moody and overly emotional? Should parents just look the other way and hope their children will outgrow it?

The short answer is no. Between 10 and 15 percent of children and adolescents have some symptoms of depression, and 13 percent of nine- to seventeen-year-olds experience some form of anxiety disorder. Overall, 5 to 7 percent of nine- to seventeen-year-olds have been diagnosed with major depression, but depression is much higher in certain subgroups of young people. Remarkably, almost 1 in 4 *suburban* middle school and high school girls have been clinically depressed. Anxiety disorders in children include persistent separation anxiety—children who, long past preschool, find it difficult to be away from parents; generalized anxiety—children who seem to worry about everything; and social phobia, or fear of being embarrassed in social situations. Obsessive-compulsive disorder affects 2 percent of teens. Added together, 1 in 5 children and teens has struggled with their mental health, a percentage that mirrors the proportion of adults with these disorders.

The U.S. Centers for Disease Control's Youth Risk Behavior Study asks middle school and high school students about feelings of depression and suicide. It was surprising and disturbing to learn that in 2003, almost one-third of seventh through twelfth graders reported that during the previous twelve months, they had "felt so sad or hopeless almost every day for two weeks or more in a row that they stopped doing some usual activities." That rate has not changed since 1999, the first year the question was asked.

Depression can be fatal. Suicide is the third leading cause of death among young people ages ten to twenty-four. A surprisingly high 17 percent of seventh through twelfth graders report that they have seriously considered attempting suicide during the past twelve months—a sobering statistic, although down dramatically and steadily from 1991's 29 percent. Girls are almost twice as likely to have considered suicide than boys are, but still, more than one in ten boys has thoughts about killing himself. Boys are four times more likely than girls to succeed in killing themselves when they do try.

Suicidal thoughts can be part of the melodramatic style of preteens, of course, but they should always be taken seriously. I have only once thought about killing myself; I was in the eighth grade and had learned that the boy I liked did not like me anymore.

I considered slitting my wrists and leaving the blood for him in a pail. Yes, very dramatic. I called a friend, who came right over. She brought a gallon of chocolate ice cream and by the time we had finished it, I was better. My parents never knew. (Well, now they do.)

For some teens, who don't yet understand the finality of death, dramatic overtures may result in death. Three percent of teens attempt suicide each year. Among them, 1,300 ten- to fourteen-year-olds and almost 20,000 fifteen- to twenty-four-year-olds are successful. The leading reasons are depression, the end of a romantic relationship, and being gay or lesbian and fearing rejection. Sometimes teenage suicides happen in what professionals call suicide clusters. One teenager commits suicide, and shortly thereafter several more in the same community follow suit. These teenagers usually have been seriously depressed already, but it is often the media and school attention on the person who committed suicide first that provokes the attempts that follow.

Parents often miss the signs of depression, and too often do not seek help for depressed children and youth. In one study, parents sought help for fewer than 1 in 20 girls and fewer than 1 in 10 boys who had depressive symptoms.

Here are some of the signs of depression. They seem hard to miss, but they are easily mislabeled as expected behaviors of teenagers. If your children exhibit any of these behaviors or a combination of behaviors for two weeks or more, you will want to have them evaluated by a qualified mental health professional.

- Are they crying excessively or do they seem persistently sad?
- Do they lack enthusiasm or motivation for activities that they once enjoyed?
- Do they suffer from chronic fatigue or a lack of energy or, conversely, do they seem unusually agitated and irritable?
- Are they withdrawing from family and friends?
- Are they gaining or losing weight or sleeping much more or much less than usual?
- Are they complaining of frequent headaches or stomachaches, or a lack of ability to concentrate?

These symptoms might be transitory. It is not unusual for pre-teens and teens to have mood swings. What you are looking for is a change in your child's behaviors and whether these changes are fleeting or lasting. Of course, these could also be symptoms of other medical problems, but it is always a good idea to have a child with these symptoms checked out by a trained mental health professional.

Parents today face a new problem when it comes to dealing with children with mental health issues, as well as some of the learning disabilities: whether it is appropriate to place them on the medications that have been created since we were children, some of which were first developed for adults.

ARE OUR CHILDREN OVERMEDICATED?

Two of my friends recently told me over the same weekend that they were considering asking doctors to place their children on medication. One is the father of a fifth-grade boy who was not turning in his homework and seemed to be having trouble concentrating in class. The other is a mother of a tenth-grade girl who is not as happy as she once was. It seems that every other child and teenager is taking something.

But the truth is that they're not, despite statements like this one from the the Uplift program, a program dedicated to increasing optimism in young people: "Pharmacology has been replacing adequate parenting as the preferred means of raising kids in the United States." In reality, most studies show that under 10 percent of the children under the age of eighteen are on some type of psychotropic medication. One study did find that the use of medication in children and teens has been going up 10 percent annually. A Harvard University study found that antidepressant use was up 64 percent in 2002, compared to 1998, among preschoolers. Yes, you read that right: preschoolers. In some cases, children are being prescribed multiple medications, although there is no good research on how the medications may interact with each other in children and youth.

According to some psychiatrists who are concerned about the overuse of prescription medicines to control children's behavior, it is "not uncommon to find a child on an anti-depressant, a mood stabilizer, and a sleep agent all at the same time." But again, reverse the statistic: more than 90 percent of children are not on these medications.

One possible reason for the recent increases is that in 1997, the Food and Drug Administration began to allow pharmaceutical companies to advertise directly to the public. Looking at recent issues of parenting magazines, I found advertisements aimed at parents for such medications as Ritalin, AdderallXR, and Concerta. Only the United States and New Zealand allow such advertising directly to consumers, although there is no question that such ads help sales. One study found that 1 in 5 adult patients now requests their medications by name. Parents should definitely be wary of doing so for their children. I recently heard a story on NPR's *All Things Considered* about a four-year-old who asked his doctor about Levitra (a medication for erectile dysfunction heavily advertised on television) when he went there for an earache. Somehow he had absorbed the message "Talk to your doctor about Levitra," not understanding that he was not the intended audience!

There is no question that for some children and teens, medications are a godsend. These young people and their families see a dramatic improvement in the quality of life after they are prescribed. But these drugs are not a panacea, they do not work for all children, and they do have side effects (which can often be controlled with changes in dosage or a switch to another medication).

In 2006, an advisory committee of the Food and Drug Administration recommended that Ritalin carry a warning, although ultimately this was downgraded to advising parents and doctors about side effects to watch out for in children, particularly related to cardiovascular disease. Although the Surgeon General concluded in the 2001 report on mental health that there are no safety issues when such drugs are used for a fourteen-month period, there simply are no long-term studies of the safety of some of these medications when used with children. Many antidepressants are now required to add a warning of a potential risk of suicide ideation in children and adolescents on their labels and in their advertisements. Some professionals are concerned that the use of these medications in children may lead to an increase in depressive symptoms in adulthood, but there is hardly consensus about that.

WHAT AFFIRMING PARENTS CAN DO

1. Have your child evaluated.

The most important thing you can do if you are concerned about a child's mental health, behavior problems, or learning issues is to have him or her carefully evaluated by a board-certified psychiatrist who specializes in children and adolescents. A pediatrician can do the medical workup on your child, but generally does not have enough training or experience to make a definitive mental health diagnosis or work up a treatment plan. And get a second opinion. ADHD is thought to be the most misdiagnosed pediatric mental disorder, and too many general pediatricians put children on medications without evaluations by highly trained and experienced mental health professionals.

Get a recommendation for a good child psychiatrist, and go in to the evaluation with an open mind. Do not go with a preconceived idea about which medication your child should be on, or with a strong feeling that he or she either should or shouldn't be on medication. Parents who demand medications and parents who resist medications are both problems, according to Dr. Susan Finkelstein, an outstanding child and teen psychiatrist in Connecticut. Dr. Finkelstein says that the most important question to ask yourself (and your child or teen) in deciding about medication is whether the symptoms of the disease are interfering with his or her functioning in life.

2. Involve your child in the conversation.

Dr. Finkelstein also strongly recommends that you involve your child and teens in these conversations. "Often the child has the best idea about whether medication is necessary or not," she says.

Dr. Finkelstein notes that, in her experience, today's upper–elementary school children through adolescents are much more accustomed to the idea that some people need medications to cope successfully in life. She reports that often she hears children as young as nine or ten discussing in her waiting room which medications they have tried, and that their siblings and friends are not uncomfortable with it. Greg reports that it's no big deal for children to visit the school or camp nurse for their medications. It may be that the stigma of brain disorders and mental illnesses is lessening in this generation; Dr. Finkelstein said to me poignantly, "It is very sad to me that among adults, the brain still isn't considered just like any other organ of the body when it comes to illnesses. Perhaps today's children and teens will change that."

3. Ask questions before agreeing to medicate your child.

The National Institutes of Mental Health suggests that you ask your mental health provider the following questions before deciding to put your child on medication:

- Do the benefits of the medication outweigh the risks?
- What are the side effects of the medication?
- What are the nonmedication alternatives?
- Will behavioral management or therapy be part of the treatment program? (For almost all mental health issues, therapy is an important adjunct to medication.)
- How often will my child's use of medication be monitored and evaluated?
- Has the drug been approved by the FDA for use in children, or are there published research studies that indicate it is effective for off-label use?

4. Get support.

It can be very stressful to have a child with any type of serious physical or emotional issue. It can definitely affect your ability to parent in the most effective ways, as stress takes its toll on you and your family. Seek opportunities for family counseling and support. There is a list of mental health resources in the Appendix that may be helpful.

Of course, parenting at times is stressful for most of us. And in my experience, the three greatest concerns many parents have for children age eight and up are sex, alcohol, and other drugs. Let's talk first about sexuality.

TEST YOUR FEAR FACTOR

1. Compared to 1971, the average age a teenager first
   has sexual intercourse is:
   a. One year earlier.
   b. Two years earlier
   c. Three years earlier.

2. The teenage birth rate was highest in:
   a. 1957.
   b. 1972.
   c. 1999.

3. Compared to a decade ago, the percentage of girls and
   boys who have performed and received oral sex has:
   a. Increased.
   b. Decreased.
   c. Stayed about the same.

4. Compared to fifteen years ago, the percent of sexually
   active young people who use contraception has:
   a. Increased.
   b. Decreased.
   c. Stayed about the same.

5. Compared to fifteen years ago, the percentage of teens
   who use condoms is:
   a. Up.
   b. Down.
   c. The same.

* * * * *
Answers: 1. a; 2. a; 3. c; 4. a; 5. a.

CHAPTER 6

Just Say Know: Raising Sexually Healthy Children

CONCERN, EVEN ALARM, over our children's sexual behavior is not new. In the 1950s, parents worried about the influence of Elvis Presley and Little Richard shaking their hips on national television. Ken Burns's excellent PBS documentary on jazz quoted an article from a 1922 issue of *New York American*, based on an Illinois Vigilance Association report: "Moral disaster is coming to hundreds of young American girls through the pathological, nerve-irritating, sex-exciting music of jazz orchestras."

Those "young American girls" were our great-grandmothers.

Despite the good news that I will share in these next two chapters about decreasing risk taking for today's kids, the fact remains that by the end of senior year in high school, more than 60 percent of young people will have drunk alcohol, more than 60 percent will have had penile-vaginal intercourse, more than half will have had oral sex, and just under half will have used at least one drug illegally. (There's a good chance you engaged in these behaviors while you were in high school as well.)

Affirming Parenting can increase the chances that your teenagers will not drink, do drugs, or have sex before they, and you, are ready. Affirming Parents know that they need to be talking to their children about these issues *before* the teenage years. They look for "teachable moments" to give their children small bits of information and to share their family values.

I've written two books about talking with your children and teenagers about sexuality issues. The overarching messages in both books are (1) talk with your children about sexuality in small teachable moments rather than having a single "big talk," and (2) be sure to talk with your children about your values about sexuality; don't just give them information.

FACT vs. FEAR

For the past ten years or so, I have received one to two calls a month from some reporter or other who wants to talk about the "oral sex epidemic among teenagers." When I ask what prompted the call, they usually tell me some version of having heard of a high school or middle school party, bar mitzvah, or school bus trip where young people are said to have been performing and receiving oral sex. When I ask if they have actually talked to a young person who was at the event and who actually witnessed the oral sex going on, the answer is generally no.

Two urban legends about teens and oral sex have been gaining popularity in the last five years. One has to do with "rainbow parties" and one has to do with jelly bracelets. At a rainbow party, girls allegedly put on a distinct color of lipstick and put their mouth on a boy's penis to leave a lipstick ring. As the story goes, the boy's goal is to get as many girls as possible to leave different colored lipstick rings on his penis.

Perhaps there are some young people who have engaged in such behavior, but in all my talks to teens around the United States about sexual decision making, I have yet to meet one. I have asked hundreds of teens if they have ever been to a rainbow party, and they all say they haven't. These young people think nothing of asking me very personal questions, from how to have or give an orgasm to detailing their first time, so I believe they would not be embarrassed to tell the truth. Should we be surprised by their answers? Does this sound like a sexually pleasurable activity for either the boy or the girl?

The jelly bracelet idea is equally unfounded. As you no doubt know, many young people today wear Lance Armstrong yellow "Livestrong" bracelets and many other colors of bracelet to bring awareness to things such as AIDS, breast cancer, domestic violence, and so on. But this story has teens wearing bracelets to let each other know how far they would like to go sexually. A girl wearing one color will only kiss; a girl with a different color band is willing to have her breasts touched; a different color band indicates a willingness to have oral sex, anal sex, and so on. Again, I have never met a teen who claimed to have done this, or heard from a teacher that it really happened.

What *do* we know for sure about young people and sex? Let's start with middle school and oral sex. There have never been any national research studies on oral sex in middle school. Think about it for a moment: How likely would your school board be to give permission for a researcher to come into your local middle school and ask twelve- and thirteen-year-olds about fellatio and cunnilingus? But it is more than a matter of squeamishness on the part of parents that has prohibited this research. In 1992, the U.S. Senate denied federal funding for an "American Teenage Study of Adolescent Sexual Behaviors," calling it a "reprehensible sex survey" and effectively limiting research on young teens for the last fifteen years.

What we know about oral sex and teens comes from young people ages fifteen to nineteen who participated in a government survey called the National Survey of Family Growth. The survey had no questions about oral sex until 2002, but there are data for young men from 1995 and 1988 from another national study called the National Survey of Adolescent Males. I'll go into this in greater depth, but let's cut to the bottom line to alleviate some of the anxiety and to challenge some of the media stories: high-quality national studies have found that even among high school juniors and seniors, almost half (45 percent) of all teens have not had oral sex.

Let me share a little bit about these studies. The first national published studies of boys were done with young men in 1988 and 1995. Remember that 1995 was two years before what I often call the 1990s' national teachable moment about oral sex. We all remember being bombarded with media stories about Monica Lewinsky, the White House intern, performing fellatio on the president of the United States and he, on at least one occasion, ejaculating on her blue Gap dress. There were endless stories in the media,

a Special Prosecutor report, and ultimately the vote for impeach-
ment. Television anchors routinely used the words *penis, oral sex,*
and *semen* early in the morning and during the evening news that
plays during the dinner hour.

Former president Bill Clinton is often blamed in media stories
for the increase in oral sex among teenagers. But there was basically
no difference in the oral sex behaviors of boys between 1995 and
2002. In both years, about half the boys had received oral sex, and
just under 4 in 10 had performed it. And what about the girls? No
one thought it was either important or appropriate to ask teenage
girls about their involvement with oral sex until 2002. At my parent
talks, it's not unusual for a woman in the audience to raise her hand
and say something like, "As a feminist, I am very concerned about
these girls performing oral sex on boys and not receiving any pleasure. What does it mean that these girls are servicing boys?" It may be
that when we were younger, it was more likely that girls gave rather
than received, but it is not true today among high school–age girls.
A little more than half of teenage girls report receiving oral sex and
slightly fewer have been the giver, percentages that are statistically
identical to teenage boys. (This might not be true in middle school,
but again, because scientists are not allowed to do such research, we
simply do not know.)

What were *we* likely to be doing with regard to oral sex when
we were in high school? The earliest data I could find was published
in 1985. Two studies found that between one-quarter and one-half
of teens had had oral sex. A smaller study in the early 1980s found
that one-quarter of teen virgins in 1982 had had oral sex, the same
percentage of virgins who had done so in the 2002 study. In other
words, despite what you may have read in the papers or heard at the
PTA meeting, there has been no change in the percentage of teens
having some type of oral sex over the past twenty years, and the proportion is pretty similar to what today's parents were doing as teens
themselves.

Although we do not have any scientific data about oral sex in
middle school, we do have age-trend data that give us strong reason
to believe that the "middle school epidemic" is primarily an epidemic of media stories and parent gossip. Only 4 in 10 fifteen- to

seventeen-year-olds report that they have had oral sex. If even as many as half of those young people began oral sex before high school, that would mean fewer than 2 in 10 middle schoolers have had this experience.

That squares with my impressions of the young people I have taught in religious education programs in churches and temples. There are usually one or two young people in a group who in one way or another let me know that they are sexually involved. The vast majority of eighth graders I have taught are more worried about kissing, and how to know if they really like someone and if someone likes them, than are considering this kind of mature sexual behavior for themselves. I can remember the name of the girl in my eighth grade who was offering oral sex to the ninth-grade athletes; I wonder if you can remember her name in your school. Today, there may be three of her instead of one. Feminist concerns to the contrary, at least in studies published way back when some of us were teens, girls are more likely to have received oral sex than given it.

Where do these stories of oral sex parties in middle school come from? The first news stories appeared in the *New York Times* in 1997 and 2000 and the *Washington Post* in 1999, which named oral sex in middle school an "unsettling new fad." Other stories of oral sex at bar mitzvahs, school dances, and school bus rides followed. More recently, even the austere *Atlantic Monthly* ran an article cleverly titled "Are You There, God? It's Me, Monica." A 1999 *Frontline* TV documentary, *The Lost Children of Rockdale County*, told the story of an oral syphilis outbreak among middle schoolers in Georgia, who were having oral sex at unchaperoned parties. Please note that these thirteen-year-olds were attending *unchaperoned* parties.

Several times a year, I am contacted by a school or a faith community about an "oral sex outbreak" among their early adolescents. As I talk more with the young people involved, I usually find out that the activity happened when the young people were in unsupervised groups for long periods of time, such as unchaperoned parties, coed church sleepovers, or school picnics or camping trips in wooded places. In almost every case, a majority of the young people are *not* involved as participants, but are only witnesses. One friend breaks a confidence and rumors start to fly. When I talk to the teens in these schools or programs about the importance of good sexual decision making and the risks of oral sex, I almost always also ask to talk with the leaders and the parents about the need to actively chaperone their children's activities.

There *is* a group of middle schoolers, about one-tenth of them, who can politely be described as "sexual adventurers," and many of them are quite open about their experiences. One in ten is a lot if it's *your* thirteen-year-old son or daughter. Indeed, some subgroups of young people enjoy a certain panache when other teens know about their sexual experiences. I remember one school official telling me that the girls who had had oral sex created a membership card and "inducted" new members after weekend parties. This subgroup may put overt pressure on other young people to join them in this behavior.

But it also happens that the middle school girl who is known to have performed oral sex, even once, may quickly get a reputation that may lead to more requests for oral sex, and she may be verbally harassed for her behaviors. I have spent time with several young women who performed oral sex, often for a popular boy, as a way to get attention and affection. It often backfires; he tells a few of his friends, they tell more boys, and the girl is painfully ostracized. Rather than becoming more popular, she gets labeled as a "ho" or "dirty." Parents may or may not find out that this has happened, but may notice changes in their daughter's satisfaction with school or social life.

I'm not saying it couldn't happen, but I have never been asked to counsel a middle school boy who's been involved in oral sex. The double standard is still alive and well in our middle schools and high schools. In fact, it's not at all uncommon for schools to ask me and my sex educator colleagues to meet with just the girls who were involved in an "oral sex" incident; I always insist on meeting with both the boys and the girls.

Despite the impression that the media sometimes give about today's teens' sexual sophistication, there has not been much change in the rates of penile-vaginal sexual intercourse since most of us were teenagers. Let's remember that it was the older baby boomers who proclaimed, "Make love, not war," although they meant on college campuses. It was the younger baby boomers and Gen Xers (today's parents of teens) who made teenage sexual intercourse the statistical norm. Between 1971 and 1979, the percentage of teenagers having sexual intercourse increased by two-thirds. In 1970, the average age for first intercourse for boys was seventeen, and for girls it was eighteen. Today, the average age is sixteen for boys and seventeen for girls. But that one-year difference *seems* like a lot because it's the difference between teens beginning to have intercourse while they are in high school and still living in our homes and beginning (for many) while away at college. As one mom told me, "I'm not sure how I feel about my seventeen-year-old son having sex with his girlfriend, but I sure don't want him doing it upstairs while I'm making dinner!"

Most teenagers do not seem to feel pressured by their peers to have sexual intercourse, despite what much of the public thinks and the media report. More than 9 in 10 young people in a 2003 poll said that being a virgin in high school is a good thing, and three-quarters say that teens are supported if they choose to wait to have sex. Teens may actually feel less pressure to have sex than teens felt fifteen to twenty years ago, and more of them say that they feel good about their decisions, whether they wait or whether they have intercourse. Popular culture has become more supporting of teens abstaining, and parent communication about waiting is making a difference. Research studies show that when teenagers report having had explicit discussions with a parent about waiting to have sex, they are more likely to delay their first time.

Despite periodic media reports of a growing callousness among teens about sexual relationships, most teenagers are waiting until they are in important romantic relationships before having intercourse. In a study of the "first time," more than 8 in 10 sexually experienced teens say that they waited until it was the right time; three-quarters said that they had been dating their partner for a long time and felt he or she was the "right person"; and 69 percent said that they were in love when they first had penile-vaginal intercourse. Casualness about sexual behaviors does not extend to sexual intercourse for most teenagers.

It's sad to report, though, that some young teens who report having had intercourse were forced into it by older teens, adults, or even family members. Significant numbers of these young people are not having sex voluntarily, but rather they report being victims of abuse. (I will talk about preventing sexual abuse in chapter 8.)

GOOD NEWS

What has changed—and this is very good news—is the proportion of teenagers who are having intercourse and the proportion among that group who use contraception. There has been a steady decline since 1991 in the percentage of teens having sexual intercourse, although it is beginning to level off. In 1991, 54 percent of high school students had had sexual intercourse; in 2005, it was 47 percent. That is not a huge decrease, but it has been steady, especially among teenage boys, whose rates of sexual intercourse have dropped 10 percent during the past fifteen years.

The gender gap for involvement in sexual intercourse is closing, and the double standard is easing; girls and boys are now virgins in about the same proportion, while boys previously had higher rates of sexual intercourse than girls. And again, despite periodic erroneous media pronouncements that teenagers are having sex at younger and younger ages, the percentage of kids under the age of thirteen who have had penile-vaginal intercourse has declined from 10 percent in 1991 to 6 percent today. Sexual intercourse among thirteen- and fourteen-year-olds has gone down as well in the past decade: fewer than 1 in 6 teens have intercourse before fifteen, compared with 1 in 5 in 1995.

Contraception use is up significantly among young people compared to 1991, and even more so compared to when we were teenagers. Trend data collected since the 1980s found that among young people who first had intercourse between 1980 and 1989, 4 in 10 did not use *any* contraceptive method; among those who did, fewer than 4 in 10 used a condom. Today, 80 percent of teens use a birth control method the first time they have sexual intercourse, nearly double the rates twenty years ago. The U.S. Centers for

Disease Control says today's teen is "much more likely to be protected at first intercourse than their counterparts having first sex before
1990."

The dramatic increase in teen condom use is a true public
health education success story that should be making media headlines. From 1980 to 1991, only 4 in 10 sexually active teens reported
that they used a condom, despite the public and press attention to
AIDS in the mid- to late 1980s. But today, more than 6 in 10 teens
(63 percent) say that they used a condom the last time they had intercourse, and almost 7 in 10 did so at first intercourse. This is a dramatic and very positive change over fifteen years ago, and two to three
times higher than it was than in the 1970s, when some of us were
teenagers.

Because of this improved and increased teen contraceptive and
condom use, teenage pregnancy, teenage births, and teenage abortion rates are down. Way down. According to the nonprofit organization Child Trends, which studies adolescent pregnancy, the pregnancy rate for teen girls is 40 per 1,000 teen girls, down from a peak
of 62 per 1,000 in 1991. In fact, the government announced in
February 2007 that the teen birth rate in the United States is at its
lowest rate in the past sixty-five years, when data began to be collected. The Guttmacher Institute, another nonprofit research organization that studies reproductive health, estimates that 85 percent of
the reason teen pregnancy rates are falling is because of improved
contraceptive and condom use; only 15 percent of the decline is
from the reduction in teenage involvement in sexual intercourse. (I
do not want to imply, though, that teenage pregnancies in the U.S.
are no longer a problem. There are about 831,000 pregnancies each
year to people aged fifteen to nineteen, and although the majority
are to those eighteen and nineteen, for too many young women
these pregnancies curtail their future employment and education
options.)

Rates of most sexually transmitted diseases (STDs) have fallen
as well, although comparing years is difficult because of changes in
the surveillance systems, as well as improved detection and screening. Consistent condom use is protective against most but not all

STDs; condom use significantly decreases transmission of human immunodeficiency virus (HIV) , the virus that causes AIDS, as well as chlamydia, gonorrhea, herpes, syphilis, and human papilloma virus. Nevertheless, STD rates are still at very high levels for today's teenagers and young adults; 1 in 4 sexually active teens contracts an STD each year, and an alarming 1 in 2 sexually active people will have at least one STD by the time they reach the age of twenty-five. The U.S. Centers for Disease Control estimates that there are 9.1 million cases of STDs each year among young people ages fifteen to twenty-four, and almost 5,000 new cases of HIV infection to young people in this age group.

Teen sexual behavior understandably concerns parents, but try to remember the good news: fewer teens are having sexual intercourse than teens were a decade ago; there is no oral sex epidemic; and contraception and condom use is up. Way up. But there are new challenges parents need to know about.

WHAT'S NEW ABOUT TEEN SEXUALITY

Do you remember the "bases"? First base was kissing, second base was touching breasts, third base was touching genitals, and going home was intercourse. Moving through the bases might take months and generally reflected how serious the relationship was getting. Sexual behaviors were tied to relational intimacy and commitment. And although it may have been frustrating at times, it gave us the chance to learn what felt good, what was pleasurable, how to kiss well, and that sexual arousal can be exciting when it's prolonged.

The "bases" that you may have grown up with do not exist in many teen worlds today. If teens are going to do more than kiss, many move quickly to some type of intercourse, behaviors that they may not be emotionally or morally ready for and that place them at risk. We need to help teenagers slow down their sexual behaviors by learning which behaviors are pleasurable, age-appropriate, and free of the risks of pregnancy and disease.

From "Hooking Up" to "Friends with Benefits"

Not only are the bases a sign of a long-ago era, but dating as we knew it has been replaced by "going together," "friends with benefits," and "hooking up."

In case these terms are new to you, "hooking up" is what may have been known as "making out" when we were younger. There is no research to suggest that it is more common today than when we were teenagers. Like then, it means engaging in sexual behaviors, which may range from heavy kissing to fondling but rarely intercourse, with someone who may or may not be a romantic partner. For some young people, it may mean oral sex, but that's probably a small minority. "Hooking up" generally means no expectations of a romantic relationship or even a repeat of the encounter; think of it as an adolescent one-night stand.

"Friends with benefits" is sexual pleasuring—again, generally not intercourse—with someone who is already a friend, not a romantic partner. Teens tell me it is for when you are not involved with anyone, but find yourself at a party, aroused or curious.

This behavior may sound callous to an adult reader, but I'm not sure it's so different from what many of us did as teenagers. I had only one steady boyfriend during my time in high school, and then for only six months; otherwise I loved to date as many boys as I could get to ask me out. Lots of those evenings ended with long kissing sessions at the beach; most did not lead to ongoing romantic relationships. "Serial dating" may not sound as stark as "hooking up," and perhaps a movie or dinner was involved in the 1970s, but it was still adolescent sexual experimentation. Just like thirty years ago, most teens are reserving their more intense sexual experiences for their boyfriends and girlfriends.

The problem, of course, with "hooking up" and "friends with benefits," or even with making out in a car at the beach, is that sexual behaviors (long before intercourse of any kind) can lead to much more complicated feelings than originally intended. I often ask the young people I teach if they have ever heard of a hooking-up situation where one of the partners discovers the next day that he or she wants more of a relationship, and sits around hoping to get a phone call or e-mail message saying, "I like you. Can we get together again?" They always say yes. Dr. Helen Fisher, who studies how our brains respond to love and lust, warns adults to be careful about having intercourse with people on a casual basis because the biochemistry of the brain may cause one to feel in love afterward. She writes in her book *Why We Love*: sexual activity can "elevate levels of dopamine and norepinephrine as well as suppress levels of serotonin. The hormone of sexual desire can trigger the release of the brain's elixirs for romantic passion...that is why it is dangerous to copulate with someone with whom you do not wish to become involved. Although you intend to have casual sex, you might just fall in love." Teens need to understand this idea as well.

Abstinence, Oral Sex, and Virginity

Even though only a small percentage of middle schoolers are having oral sex, today's middle schooler is much more likely to *know* about oral sex than many of us did when we were in the seventh grade. But some of these kids give an impression that they are far more sophisticated than they really are. When I was doing research for my book on teenagers and sex, I held focus groups of teens and asked them about sexual games at parties. One asked me if I knew about a game called "Suck and Blow." It's not what it sounds like. During the game, young people sit in a circle and pass a playing card from mouth to mouth. One person blows on the card and the other person sucks in to catch it. The game is fun because it often doesn't work: when the card drops, the two people have to kiss. The name of this game is an example of how teens often act sophisticated about what they know, when what they know may be less than they think.

There is also a generational issue here. Many of today's adults didn't have oral sex until after they had intercourse, and cunnilingus in particular may not have been among the skills of many boys when we were in high school. Although most people over thirty I talk to believe that oral sex is more intimate than intercourse, people under thirty tend to believe that it is less so. But once again, it was the baby-boom generation that changed mores about oral sex. Although only about 15 percent of those born between 1933 and

1942 reported that they had ever had oral sex, over 80 percent of men and women born between 1948 and 1962 had.

It should not surprise us that some teenagers are experimenting with oral sex. Not only is there more discussion and openness about oral sex in the culture today, but a new federal program promoting abstinence from sexual intercourse until marriage may also ironically be contributing to oral sex among teens. These initiatives, which began in 1997 and have cost more than half a billion dollars to date, require federally funded programs to teach teens that they are expected to be virgins when they get married. Specifically, the law requires teaching that a "mutually faithful monogamous relationship in the context of marriage is the expected standard of human sexual activity," and that sexual activity before marriage is "likely to have harmful psychological and physical effects." Yes, those are the *exact* requirements for programs receiving funds from this federal program.

Some young people absorbing these messages may not give up sex, just intercourse. In one study of teens who had taken virginity pledges, a standard offering of some of the abstinence-only programs, they were four times as likely to have had oral sex and six times more likely to have had anal sex than teens who did not take the pledge. They may report to researchers, their parents, and their religious leaders that they are virgins, but they certainly are not sexually inexperienced. One has to wonder if the proponents of abstinence programs are comfortable with the result that teens are engaging in more mouth-to-genital and penile-anal contact. According to a study published in 2006 in the *American Journal of Public Health*, more than half the young people who said they took virginity pledges in an initial survey denied a year later that they had done so. Among these deniers, three-quarters had broken the pledge and had had sexual intercourse a year later. So much for program efficacy.

Whoa, you may be thinking, how can young people consider oral and anal sex "abstinence"? The fact is that these programs often are not very clear about how to be abstinent (except for not having penile-vaginal intercourse until marriage), and in several studies teens have said that oral sex is not sex. Indeed, in one widely quoted study from 1999 in the prestigious *Journal of the American Medical Association*, nearly 6 in 10 college students (59 percent) said that they did not consider people who had "just" had oral-genital contact to have had sex. (An interesting side note: the decision to publish this article cost the editor of the journal his job. It was seen as too political.)

In other words, just as when many of us were growing up, teens think one can still be a virgin as long as a penis does not enter a vagina. You may remember President Clinton saying he was not lying when he said, "I did not have sexual relations with that woman" and his paltry defense that it depends on what "it" is. But you and I, and probably even our parents, grew up with that exact same sexual ethic. When I was in high school, "nice" girls did not do "it," but it was considered acceptable to do what we labeled "everything but" with a steady boyfriend. In a Gallup poll of adults during the height of the Clinton/Lewinsky coverage, 20 percent of the adults agreed that oral sex is not really sex. For some teenagers, engaging in oral sex may be a way to practice abstinence and thereby comply with their parents', teachers', and religious institution's hopes for them.

Nora Gelperin, a sexuality educator at ANSWER, a national teen hotline at Rutgers University, studies oral sex in young people and writes that "some girls even feel empowered during oral sex as the only sexually behavior in which they have complete control of their partner's pleasure." She told me that teens see oral sex as less intimate than intercourse because the partners do not have to be nude, no eye contact is expected, it maintains virginity, it does not risk pregnancy, it can be over quickly, and it is less risky for sexually transmitted diseases. In one study of teenage girls by the Kaiser Family Foundation and *Seventeen* magazine, a third of fifteen- to seventeen-year-old girls reported having oral sex as a way to avoid losing their virginity. In another study of ethnically diverse ninth graders from California, teens reported that oral sex, compared to penile-vaginal intercourse, was "less risky, more prevalent, and more acceptable." They said teens who engage in oral sex are less likely to get a "reputation," to get in trouble, to feel bad about themselves, or to feel guilty.

Some teenagers self-identify as virgins because they are experimenting with same-sex sexual relationships and thus penile-vaginal intercourse is not part of their sexual repertory. The average age when young people are "coming out" appears to be younger than it was for people our age, although there are not many good studies on this (again, because of the political difficulty of asking the question; for example, the Youth Risk Behavior Survey does not ask students whether their sexual activity took place with a partner of the same sex or the other sex). One study of adult gay people in 1981 found that males first acted on their homosexual feelings at the age of about fifteen, while lesbians reported an average age of twenty. Until the mid-1990s, most gay people did not come out until adulthood. Today, according to studies conducted by the Gay, Lesbian, Straight Education Network, approximately 5 percent of America's high school students identify as gay or lesbian, with the average gay teen self-identifying between the ages of fifteen and seventeen. Although these studies are not directly comparable and coming out is a process, not a distinct act, many experts believe that today's gay adolescents are more likely to accept their sexual orientation and tell others earlier than teens would have twenty years ago.

STDs

Alarmingly, but mirroring adult behavior, many teenagers are not protecting themselves against sexually transmitted diseases during oral sex and a quarter aren't during penile-vaginal intercourse. In the National Survey of Family Growth, fewer than 1 in 10 young people say they use protection when they are having oral sex. In a study of religious teens, 55 percent did not know that a person can get a "sexually transmitted disease from unprotected oral sex." Yes, herpes, gonorrhea, chlamydia, human papilloma virus, hepatitis B, and syphilis can be transmitted through oral sex, and there is a small risk of HIV transmission as well.

Knowledge about the widespread prevalence of sexually transmitted diseases is definitely one of the changes since we were teenagers. For those of us who came of age sexually in the 1970s, the only sexually transmitted diseases most of us knew about were syphilis and gonorrhea, and they were both curable. Today we know that there are (and have always been) many sexually transmitted diseases. My son recently stumped his dad at dinner when he brought up something he had learned in his eighth-grade health class: "Dad, what's the most common STD?" he asked. Ralph answered, "Syphilis." Greg told him to guess again, and Ralph answered, "Herpes." When Greg told him it was chlamydia, Ralph confessed that he wasn't even sure what its symptoms were.

Human papilloma virus, trichimoniasis, and chlamydia account for 88 percent of all STDs in young adults aged fifteen to twenty-four, but sexually active young people are also at risk for gonorrhea, syphilis, hepatitis B, bacterial vaginosis, pubic lice, molluscum contagiosum, scabies, and nonspecific urethritis. (It is likely because health education classes focus more on the dangers of sex than its pleasures that your preteen or teenager knows more about these diseases than you do; ask them.)

The first cases of AIDS were diagnosed in 1981; the virus and its transmission were first understood in 1985. Children and teenagers today were born after HIV and AIDS were facts of life, and that has affected both their understandings of their sexuality and our concerns for them. As a young woman in one of my classes said to me a few years ago, "I have always known that sex could kill me." That sounds stark to those of us who grew up during the years of the sexual revolution.

As frightening as AIDS is, we need to be at least as concerned about protecting our children from the other sexually transmitted diseases. Several common STDs have no cure, and many, like chlamydia, often have no symptoms. Your teenage children may be infected and not know it. We now know that one particular type of the human papilloma virus is responsible for cervical cancer (although most forms are not, and a new vaccine is available to protect young women from the cancer-causing kind). Untreated chlamydia may cause future infertility. At least 1 in 6 women in our generation found out through the agony of infertility treatment and testing that they had damaged their fallopian tubes during unprotected sex in earlier decades.

WHAT AFFIRMING PARENTS CAN DO

Parenting style makes a difference in teenagers' sexual decisions as well. Forbidding your tween to have a boyfriend or girlfriend may mean only that you won't know when he or she has a romantic partner. Many preteens have confided in me that they have a boyfriend or girlfriend at school, but that their parents would "kill them" if they found out. The same is true for teens. Communicating "if I ever find you carrying condoms, I will ground you for six months" means that your child is less likely to be protected, not less likely to have sex. Authoritarian parents need to understand that laying down the law when it comes to romance and sex is *not* likely to increase the chances that your children will abstain. But Affirming Parents may be more successful in knowing whether their children have a romantic partner, setting limits for where they can go and when they can be alone, and getting to know their children's romantic partner.

1. Start educating about sexuality early.

It's critical for parents to talk to their children and teens about sexuality, including contraception and the use of condoms to prevent sexually transmitted diseases *before* they're confronted with these situations—which may be sooner than you think. Affirming Parents face the possibility that their children will become sexually involved during their teenage years. And that's likely to be the case, particularly if they are in love and particularly as they approach the end of high school and the first years of college. In a study by the Society for Adolescent Medicine, more than 6 in 10 parents report being concerned about adolescent sexual behavior, but surprisingly, more than 8 in 10 didn't believe their own child was sexually involved. Facing this possibility is not the same as giving your children permission to have sexual intercourse; in fact, parental actions can contribute to helping young people delay their first time.

2. Communicate your values.

Not surprisingly, how you parent around sexuality issues and how you communicate your values about sex to your children make a difference. A study of more than twelve thousand teenagers from around the country found that in homes where parents give their preteen and teenage children clear messages that indicate that they disapprove of teenagers having intercourse, the children are more likely to postpone their first intercourse and to have fewer partners than teens who have not had those types of explicit discussions. Other studies have indicated that in homes where parents and teens talk openly about sexuality, the teen is not only more likely to wait to have intercourse but more likely to use contraception and condoms when he or she does become sexually active. For example, several studies have found that the more moms talk to their sons about birth control and condoms, the more consistently their sons will use condoms.

3. Set limits for dating.

One rule that I feel is very important is to make sure your child picks age-appropriate partners. Girls who date boys more than two years or two grade levels above them are thought to be much more likely to engage in sexual intercourse and in unprotected sex. I am guessing that is true of boys with much older girlfriends or boyfriends as well, although there is no research to back this up. Having your teens agree to the rule of dating no more than two grades apart will greatly decrease the likelihood of their involvement in sexual behaviors.

On the other hand, Permissive Parents who ignore their teens' sexuality or who let them entertain their boyfriends or girlfriends in their bedrooms with the door shut or when the adults are not home are naive to think that they aren't engaging in sexual behavior. Studies indicate that teens from both Permissive and Authoritarian homes are more likely to have intercourse earlier than those from homes where Affirming Parents talk explicitly with their children about their values about sex. Affirming Parents can communicate their value that they do not want their teens to begin intercourse in high school (or until they are in a mature relationship or engaged or married or whatever your values are), but tell them that if they do choose to have intercourse, they must protect themselves. According to many studies, teens who receive both messages are more likely to delay their first intercourse and then to protect themselves when they do have it. Educational programs with these messages have been found to be more likely to be effective in helping young people delay intercourse than abstinence-only programs.

4. Supervise and monitor.

Supervision and monitoring your preteen and teen make a difference. It should not surprise anyone that when teenagers are allowed to entertain their partners in their bedrooms with the doors closed, or go with them to unchaperoned parties, they are more likely to experiment with sexual behaviors. Teens know that time alone in the family room is likely to be interrupted by other family members, so most curtail what they will do sexually. Both "Just say no" and threats about sex—or, conversely, a "teens will be teens" attitude, coupled with little supervision—lead to higher rates of teen sexual behaviors.

Like the other areas we have discussed, a blend of jointly setting limits, having clear expectations, and supervising and monitoring makes a difference. Gay and lesbian young people may actually have more unsupervised time for sexual behaviors; because parents often assume that their children are heterosexual, they think nothing of having their son or daughter have a friend sleep over in their room or even their bed. It may be unsettling to think about, but many of my adult gay and lesbian friends report that they had their first same-sex sexual experiences during such unsuspecting sleepovers.

5. Keep talking and then talk some more.

Affirming Parents know that it is important to talk about a broad range of sexuality issues with your tweens and teenagers and to keep the dialogue open. Parents are sometimes afraid of talking about sex with their children for fear that it will make their children more likely to have sex or that talking about abstinence while bringing up birth control and condoms sends a double message. There is not a single research study that has found that adult-child communication about sexuality, whether it is from parents or teachers, causes teens to have sexual intercourse at earlier ages. In fact, just the opposite is true.

As for the concern about mixed messages, we give our children and teens mixed messages all the time. We tell our children to go out and play, but to put on sunscreen. We tell our young drivers not to speed, but to wear seat belts. We tell them not to drink, but if they do, never to drive. There's no controversy around Mothers Against Drunk Driving saying they don't "condone drinking or using other drugs—[but we] acknowledge that teens may find themselves in dangerous situations, but they do not deserve to die because of these situations."

In the case of sex, that means not facing an unintended pregnancy that could change their whole lives or a sexually transmitted disease that could harm their health, impair their fertility, or kill them. More than twenty years ago, I told the Eagle Forum's Phyllis Schlafly in a debate on a PBS program: "It is immoral to say to the young people of America, Just say no or die." As a minister, I feel that even more strongly today.

What we can do is help set the foundation in our homes that we are able and willing to talk to our children about sexuality. This begins in the earliest years of life, literally when your child is in diapers. But it is never too late to start.

6. Guide their decision making about sex.

Some of the most important things you can talk with your pre-teen and teenager about are how people know when they are ready to have sexual intercourse of any kind and how to set and maintain sexual limits. Most parents have told their children to say no, but not when they might say yes or which behaviors parents might find developmentally appropriate. First you have to think about which values you want to teach your child and teenager about sexual behaviors. Take a moment and think what you want to convey about the morality of premarital intercourse. Discuss it with your child's other parent. Do you want your child to wait until marriage to have sexual intercourse, which may mean waiting until their twenties or thirties or perhaps never having it? Are you hoping that they will graduate high school as a virgin? Do you want them to be in love or in a committed relationship? Do you have an acceptable age in mind, or is it more about the maturity of your teen and the stability of the relationship? Do you have to be happy with their choice of romantic partner, or do you trust their judgment? When you think about wanting your children to abstain from sex, what behaviors are you hoping they abstain from: French kissing? Orgasm? Genital caressing? Oral sex? Penile-vaginal intercourse? Anal sex?

Thinking through these questions will not be easy. I understand firsthand how difficult it is to contemplate your child (at any age!) being nude with a partner, no less engaging in sexual acts. I think some of the reason for the popularity of media stories about oral sex is that they play into adults' discomfort about our teens' experiencing erotic pleasure. It is next to impossible for parents, teachers, or religious educators to discuss oral sex or masturbation with young people without addressing sexual pleasure and sexual response, and most of us are not very comfortable doing that.

But that is exactly what Affirming Parents need to do. If we want our teens to wait to have any kind of intercourse until they are both emotionally and (as I discussed in the beginning of chapter 5) neurologically mature enough to handle the consequences, we need to talk to them about which sexual behaviors we think they might be able to handle. If we can talk with our middle school and high school and even college-age children about the pleasures and benefits of nonpenetrative behaviors (including masturbation), we help guide them in their sexual development. Frankly, I have talked with too many young people who moved quickly from kissing to oral sex or intercourse, skipping the sexual learning and the slowly increasing sexual intimacy that many of us remember, and then regretting it.

7. Discuss the characteristics of a moral, ethical sexual relationship.

One of the most important conversations Affirming Parents can have with their tweens and teens is about the characteristics of a moral, ethical sexual relationship. Your children need your help and guidance to think about setting and maintaining sexual limits. Whether I am working with senior adults, college or seminary students, or eighth graders at my church, I teach five criteria for a moral sexual relationship. It should be:

- Consensual
- Nonexploitative
- Honest
- Mutually pleasurable
- Protected against pregnancy and disease if any type of intercourse occurs.

I ask students to tell me how they would be able to know if these five characteristics existed, and they generally identify what I label the Three Conditions: Time (to get to know the other person), Communication (about sexual desires, the relationship, and protection), and Shared Values (what it will mean to each person if sexual behaviors occurs). I suggest to students that they memorize the five characteristics and ask themselves if all are present before they agree to move beyond kissing with a partner. I suggest more time and more communication if all five characteristics are not present or if it's unclear whether they are. I firmly believe there would be significantly less teenage involvement in sexual intercourse and oral sex if young people took the time to evaluate their relationships by these criteria; adults using them might make better sexual decisions as well.

These criteria are more ethically rigorous than simply telling young people to wait until marriage to have sexual intercourse. These criteria apply to sexual relationships before as well as after marriage. They accept no double standards and apply to all, regardless of age, disability, or sexual orientation. You may have different moral criteria based on your family values that you want to give your children, but the point is to give them guidance on setting sexual limits. If you want your children to be virgins when they marry, they still need your guidance about which behaviors you might think are appropriate and strategies for avoiding those that you do not.

It is also important to talk with your tweens and teens about how alcohol and drug use can affect their ability to make healthy decisions about sex. Almost one-quarter of high school students report that they used alcohol or drugs before the last time they had sexual intercourse. Far too many of the young people I've worked with over the years have done the same, as a way of not taking responsibility for their sexual behavior.

Of course, our concerns about children and teens drinking go well beyond worrying that it will decrease their inhibitions about sex. In the next chapter we'll explore the topic of alcohol and drugs.

TEST YOUR FEAR FACTOR

1. Compared to fifteen years ago, drinking among middle school students has:
   a. Increased.
   b. Decreased.
   c. Stayed about the same.

2. Compared to fifteen years ago, drinking among high school students has:
   a. Increased.
   b. Decreased.
   c. Stayed about the same.

3. Compared to a decade ago, binge drinking has:
   a. Increased.
   b. Decreased.
   c. Stayed about the same.

4. Compared to thirty years ago, marijuana use among teens has:
   a. Increased.
   b. Decreased.
   c. Stayed about the same.

5. The percentage of people who use marijuana and go on to have serious drug problems is:
   a. 50 percent.
   b. 25 percent.
   c. Less than 10 percent.

* * * * *

Answers: 1. b; 2. b; 3. b; 4. b; 5. c.

CHAPTER 7

Sobering News: Alcohol, Drugs, and Raising Responsible Children

As I INTERVIEWED parents for this book, one concern I heard over and over again was that drinking is out of control and that drug use was increasing among tweens and teenagers. Parents reported to me that both their middle school and high school students were under intense peer pressure to drink or get high, and that alcohol use seemed almost universal. Teenagers reported to me that "all" their friends drank, and that for many of their friends it was no big deal to "get wasted." Media stories lead parents to worry that out-of-control drinking is a new and growing problem, and that marijuana is much more dangerous today than it was in the 1960s and 1970s.

Is any of this true?

FACT vs. FEAR

As with many of the other areas I have discussed, the facts about alcohol and drug use among children seem to contradict what we hear in the media. For instance, the proportion of teenage drinking is *decreasing*, not increasing, as you may have read or heard. In 1991, half of teens reported that they had had one drink of alcohol on one or more of the preceding thirty days; in 2005, it had gone down to 43 percent, with a decline of more than 10 percentage points among boys. There was a slight decrease in the number of teens who reported their first drink (beyond a few sips) before the age of thirteen, to a low of just over one-quarter (25.6 percent). In fact, in an annual survey, the latest study found that college freshmen reported the lowest rates of drinking in *thirty-eight years!*

Young people today begin drinking about the same time that we did; just over one-quarter of the class of 1975 and one-quarter of the class of 2005 reported having had at least one drink of alcohol before the end of eighth grade. The average age that a young person today has his or her first drink is fourteen. But even among high school seniors, drinking is far from universal: fully one-quarter of twelfth graders report never having used alcohol at all, and 4 in 10 report never having been drunk.

But guess who is drinking more? Adults. Binge drinking (defined as consuming four or more drinks at one time) is up slightly among adults; and 6 percent of American adults are now considered by the Centers for Disease Control to be chronic drinkers (having an average of two or more drinks every day), up from 3 percent in 1990. Although 6 percent may not sound like a lot, one wonders why we do not see headlines and media stories about adult drinking going up 100 percent in the past fifteen years. And no surprise: the children of regular drinkers are more likely to drink themselves and more likely to have easy access to alcohol.

It will also probably not surprise you that overall drug use was actually higher when we were teenagers than it is today. According to Monitoring the Future, the annual survey of adolescent drug and alcohol use that began in 1975, drug use went up from 1978 to 1999 but has been steadily declining since. It actually peaked at the height of the government's "Just say no" campaign, but this was also when more baby boomers were speaking publicly about their own use. Remember Bill Clinton's famous "I tried marijuana but did not inhale"? In 1976, the survey found that over half (52.8 percent) of high school seniors reported having tried marijuana; in 2005, 47.6 percent of high school seniors had tried it. In other words, *fewer* high school teens were using marijuana than when some of us were graduating from high school.

You have also surely heard the public service ads stating that marijuana is much more dangerous today then when we were teenagers. The national drug czar coined the catchy phrase "It's not your father's marijuana" in 2002, and claimed in an op-ed piece in the *Washington Post* that today's marijuana was 30 times stronger than when we were young. Others say that it is 10 to 20 times stronger. According to WebMD, the potency of marijuana is 560 percent stronger than it was in 1975. But according to the National Institute on Drug Abuse, which has funded the University of Mississippi to test the potency of seized marijuana samples for more than eighteen years, the overall potency of marijuana has increased from 2 to 4 percent and the "average levels of the active ingredient in marijuana, THC, jumped from 3.3% in 1985 to over 8% in 2005." That is a real increase, but it's not 560 percent, and it does not seem to warrant the scary headlines.

It is also largely a myth that marijuana leads to hard-core drug use. The research data show that for more than 9 in 10 people, marijuana use does not lead to either dependency or other drugs (although that proportion may be higher for young people who initiate in early adolescence). The Monitoring the Future study found that for most teens, experimentation with marijuana does not lead to an increase in other drug use or other risky behavior (although it may decrease a teen's resolve not to have sex.)

Just as when we were teenagers, some organizations use scare tactics to try to keep young people from using alcohol and drugs. Remember the ubiquitous commercial "This is your brain. This is your brain on drugs," showing an egg in a frying pan? Even the staunchest antidrug professionals have admitted that this ad did not dissuade many young people from experimenting. A frequently run TV advertisement today warns young people that sniffing household products will cause their brain to believe it is drowning; we watch a young girl squeezing her teddy bear, drowning as her room is filled with water. It does not ring true, either, but it is frightening to watch.

The Partnership for a Drug-Free America even uses scare tactics with parents. A recent full-page newspaper ad blared at the top "How to Write an Obituary for Your Teenager." It was about the dangers of teens sniffing household products. It got my attention, but quite honestly, it did not lead to a discussion with my teen about inhalants. And, of course, the ad did not bother to tell readers that inhalant use has been steadily decreasing for the past fifteen years and was at its lowest level ever in 2005. Inhalant use (sniffing glue, aerosol spray cans, paint, and the like to get high) has actually been decreasing, from a high of 20 percent in 1995 to just over 12 percent today. Still, that is more than 1 in 10 high school students engaging in a dangerous practice.

21st-CENTURY CHALLENGES

Although the numbers have gone down, the amount of young people using and abusing alcohol and other drugs is still way too high. Our generation was also plagued with a high incidence of drug and alcohol use, but there are some real differences now.

Alcohol Use

We should be very concerned that 60 percent of teenagers have been drunk at least once. The transition into middle school and from seventh to eighth grade are the most dangerous times for an increase in experimentation with alcohol. Thirteen percent of twelve-year-olds have had a drink, but that increases to a quarter of thirteen-year-olds and 37 percent of fourteen-year-olds. A disturbing 10 percent of nine- and ten-year-olds have started drinking. The transition from elementary school to middle school is an especially vulnerable time for young people, as peer pressure begins to increase. It's important to set a clear no-use rule and clear consequences if you find out that your middle school child has been drinking. It may also be the time to put a lock on your liquor cabinet, especially if your child is home alone after school or in the evenings.

But what about alcohol use among older teenagers? Dr. David J. Hanson, a sociologist and professor emeritus at the State University of New York at Potsdam, has been studying alcohol use and teens for more than twenty years. He believes that parents should be teaching young people moderation and responsible alcohol use and that, similar to abstinence-only sexuality education programs, prohibition is not likely to be effective. He says that in homes where parents abstain from all alcohol, they can certainly teach their children their values and request them to abstain as well. In homes where parents have histories of alcoholism, it may be especially important to discuss abstention because of the genetic risk of the disease.

Dr. Hanson also told me "we must become more concerned about teen *abuse* of alcohol rather than their *use* of alcohol." In other words, we need to worry much more about the quarter of young people who had five or more drinks in a row in the last month than the 4 in 10 who had one drink during the month. Driving after half a beer is probably less dangerous than driving after a night of binge drinking. Although I agree with Dr. Hanson that abuse is the greater concern, Affirming Parents will consider setting a clear no-use rule *outside of the home* for their tweens and high school–age teens. Not only does that keep your child from engaging in an illegal activity, but it also keeps them from drinking due to peer pressure and from opportunities for bingeing and overuse. It allows you to monitor their use and to teach moderation at home.

The problem is that many parents seem unwilling to set such a no-use rule outside of the home. Many parents seem to believe that teenage social drinking is a fact of life that they just have to tolerate, and that their teen will be ostracized if he or she is forbidden to go to parties and drink. In the town where my church is located, parents actually worked to defeat a proposal to increase financial consequences for teenagers found by police to be drinking alcohol at parties or in open areas. Many suburban parents tell me that they do not care if their teenagers drink as long as they don't drive; they turn a blind eye if their teenager comes home drunk after an evening out. Many of the parents I talk to seem to assume that there's nothing they can do about it. As one baby-boomer parent told me, shrugging his shoulders, "I don't like that she drinks, but that's what teenagers do today."

I have even heard of parties where parents serve alcohol to underage teens as long as they promise not to drive. The parents get the keg and then collect the car keys. Some require the teens to sleep over. (Given the relationship between drinking and sex, that's probably a recipe for pregnancy and STDs.) Other permissive parents look the other way while their teens attend or even give unchaperoned parties, where it is assumed that teens will bring and drink alcohol. In fact, some of my good friends have told me that they thought I was too strict with Alyssa when she was a teenager. I was the parent who called to make sure that there was going to be an actively chaperoning parent home during any parties. And once she began to drive, we rehearsed how she could gracefully leave a party that was getting out of control. Some parents rehearse code words with their teen children, so that a call from a cell phone that says, "Mom, I'm calling like you asked" really means, "Please come get me." Your son or daughter could also send you a text message without anyone knowing it's asking for a ride home. One teenager told me that she goes to the bathroom, pretends to be sick, and then calls her parents to pick her up when it turns out a party includes drinking.

Permitting teens unrelated to you to drink in your home gives your teen the message that you think it's okay for him or her to drink outside your home as well; but more than that, it is also illegal in most states. For example, in 2006, Connecticut passed a law making it a crime for adults to permit underage drinking on private property. Adults can now be fined $500 and up to a year in jail for permitting teens to drink in their homes, or even for looking the other way.

It should not surprise us that so many teenagers, particularly in affluent areas, drink. Dr. Suniya Luthar from Columbia University has been studying teens in affluent areas and urban centers. What she found was that teens in affluent suburbs have much higher drinking rates than young people in the inner city; compared to urban young people, they are more likely to have been drunk or to be regular drinkers.

Teenagers who drink are also much more likely to try drugs than those who don't drink. Teenage drug use correlates with other risk-taking and rebellious behaviors, but drug use is actually fairly common among all groups of teens. It may surprise you to find out that affluent teenage girls have the highest rates for substance use of any kind; compared to other teenagers, they have the highest rates of cigarette, alcohol, and marijuana use, and suburban boys have the highest rates of hard drug use. Drug use among inner-city teens is much lower. That is partially because suburban teens have more money to purchase alcohol and drugs, but several parenting experts and researchers believe the higher use is also related to suburban teens' disconnection from parents and too many expectations being placed on them for achievement. Suburban teens report more anxiety and slightly more depression than inner-city teens; these mental health issues are predictors of substance and alcohol use.

Teenagers drink or use drugs for the same reasons that adults drink or use drugs. They may do it for recreation—to experiment, for enjoyment, to bond with others, to deal with social boredom or with peer pressure. Boys may especially feel pressure to use alcohol or drugs. Contrary to the media image of the teen substance abuser as a rebel or loner, the more popular a boy is, the more likely it is that he will drink. Young people, even those in middle school, may also be self-medicating to dull their anxious or depressed feelings.

Change in the Age of Legal Drinking

Many parents my age remember being able to drink legally at eighteen. But in 1984, Congress passed the Minimum Drinking Age Act, which required every state to raise its legal drinking age to twenty-one or risk losing federal highway funds. Not surprisingly, every state complied. The United States now has the highest legal drinking age in the world. Many public health professionals and educators think that the policy has backfired; I agree.

So, although you may remember social occasions with alcohol at college (I fondly remember sherry hours with a particular professor), today's college student is more likely to be getting wasted in the dorm room before the party begins. It is called the "pre-party," and it means that many students, in both high school and college, show up at "no-alcohol" school events pretty drunk. Rather than helping young adults learn to drink in moderation over the course of a social evening, these laws encourage heavy drinking in a short period of time. Several university presidents have called for a lowering of the national drinking age to reduce binge drinking on campus and teach moderation.

That raises an interesting problem for those of us with college-age children. Many of them spend semesters abroad, where it is legal for them to drink. Many of them are on college campuses where drinking is very common. Many of us do not object to our college-age student having a glass of beer or wine with us at dinner. It seems reasonable, then, to help our almost-adult children learn to drink in moderation and to express our concerns about binge drinking. But since drinking under twenty-one is still illegal, as with every other area I have discussed, you must decide which values you want to share with your child.

Marijuana and Other Drug Use

We clearly need to address the problem that 1 in 5 high school students smokes marijuana on a regular basis. In addition, the average age of first marijuana use has gone down, and that's a cause for concern. While most of today's baby boomers first tried marijuana when they were away at college, today many students are beginning before their junior year in high school. Ten percent of young people first smoke marijuana before the age of thirteen, and early use may be particularly problematic. As with any adult behavior, if it's your middle school student who is getting high, the fact that the other 90 percent of students aren't isn't reassuring.

Another troubling new trend is that the use of substances besides marijuana has actually been increasing among young people over the past fifteen years, but the number of users is still small. In 1991, 6 percent of students had tried cocaine; in 2005, that was up to almost 8 percent. Cocaine use increased steadily from 1991 to 1999, but has been on the decline since 2001. Steroid use is up from 2.7 percent in 1991 to 4 percent in 2005.

Young people's use of prescription drugs and over-the-counter medications to get high is also increasing. While in the 1970s, kids had to turn to older friends who somehow had access to drug dealers, today's young person need look no farther than under the kitchen sink or inside their parents' medicine cabinet.

After marijuana, the second most popular illicit drugs used by teenagers are prescription drugs that have not been prescribed for them. The 2004 National Survey of Drug Use and Health found that 1 in 5 teens had used a prescription painkiller to get high, and that has dramatically increased since 1985. (But, as with other areas I have discussed, the increase in the abuse of prescription drugs is even greater among adults. Remember Rush Limbaugh?) The most common medications that teens use to get high are OxyContin, Vicodin, Demerol, Valium, Xanax, and ADHD medications like Ritalin and Dexedrine. Where are they getting these medications? From our medicine cabinets.

As with teen drinking, some young people feel comfortable using marijuana and other drugs because they have received ambivalent messages from their parents about them. More than half of baby boomers used marijuana when they were younger, and many still do, at least occasionally. I have to admit to a certain nostalgic yearning when I smell marijuana at a concert; like most people my age, I had a period in college where I got high, but it has not been part of my life for more than twenty-five years. That's pretty typical: most adolescent and college marijuana users cease all illegal drug use after a few years of experimentation.

Does "Drug Education" Work?

For the past two decades, children have been bombarded with drug education long before they turn eighteen, with mixed results (as the increase in marijuana use shows). Almost every high school in the United States addresses alcohol and other drug use with students. In my home state of Connecticut, some drug education is required every year, from kindergarten through high school. By the time my children were ten, they could list and describe any number of illegal drugs, as well as their street names. (I have always wondered who decided that this was important information for elementary school students.) Now in the eighth grade, Greg reports that the program hasn't changed much since elementary school. I remember when Alyssa was in first grade and became very upset as I poured a glass of wine for my husband and myself one Friday night to have with dinner. "Oh, Mom," she pleaded, "please don't drink. I don't want you or Daddy to be alcoholics." She had learned that in her kindergarten health class.

In fifth-grade classes around the country, young people are taking part in the DARE program: Drug Abuse Resistance Education. It is used in 80 percent of the school districts in the United States, at a cost of over a billion dollars a year. The program is taught by police officers, who spend several sessions telling the ten-year-olds not to use drugs, often relying on scare tactics. But, despite the massive financial investment of our tax dollars, the DARE program does not work. The U.S. General Accounting Office, the U.S. Surgeon General, the National Academy of Sciences, the National Institutes of Health, and the U.S. Bureau of Justice Assistance have all found that DARE is ineffective in preventing drug use among young people. In fact, studies in several states found that participation actually seemed to increase the likelihood that young people would try drugs.

But there is a "feel-good" element to these programs, and smart fifth-grade students know to give the officers positive feedback. The last assignment in Alyssa's DARE class was to write an essay on what the program meant to her. For weeks she had been complaining about what a waste of time she thought DARE was, but her letter to the officer in charge could not have been more complimentary. She told him that the program had changed her life and that she would never forget it. When I asked her why she had not been honest, she said, "Mom, I didn't want to hurt his feelings. And I didn't want to fail the class."

I am not advocating a permissive attitude toward marijuana or any other drug, just some perspective. It seems absolutely clear to me that we do not want our children altering their brain chemistry in middle school and high school, and so communicating a no-use expectation, as with alcohol, is a good idea. It is also clear that alcohol and drugs can impair your child's judgment, decision making, and likelihood to engage in other risky behaviors like sex, pranks, and driving under the influence, just as it does with adults.

There are legitimate reasons to be concerned about your tween or teen experimenting with marijuana. Various drug education Web sites present the rationale for telling your teens not to smoke marijuana: these include problems with memory, problem solving, mood swings, depression, anxiety, menstruation, and gynecomastia (breast enlargement in boys). The research on the health-compromising impact of marijuana is very compelling for the youngest adolescents. Surely we should be uncomfortable that 5 percent of eighth graders have tried marijuana. According to the American Academy of Pediatrics, heavy marijuana use during puberty may be an especially dangerous risk for infertility; it is correlated with decreased sperm counts, slower sperm motility, and irregular ovulation. The potential impact on brain development of both early alcohol and drug experimentation also seems clear: young teens have enough difficulty thinking through decisions without adding substances to further compromise their thinking or their brain development. And there is some research indicating that the earlier marijuana use begins, the more likely it is to become habit-forming.

But most of the sites about marijuana use for late teens, college students, and yes, adults, eventually admit that the true danger is frequent and long-term use, not occasional experimentation. For example, frequent long-term use, according to WebMD, can "contribute to developing some kinds of cancer, breathing problems, similar to smoking such as coughing and wheezing, and a weakened immune system," as well as heart, lung, and reproductive problems. But frequent use is defined as more than twenty days a month, which defines only a small proportion of teens who have tried the drug.

At my college reunion this year, one of my classmates, Dr. Andrea G. Barthwell, gave a talk on marijuana use and young people. She had served as the Deputy Director of the Office of National Drug Control Policy for the first Bush administration. She talked about adolescent drug use, the need for stronger drug laws, and the role parents can play. Many in the baby-boomer audience seemed skeptical about her warnings. They just did not hit home. She did say that for 9 in 10 people, marijuana did not lead to harder drugs and was not addictive for most who use it sporadically.

I asked Dr. Barthwell, given the research that recreational marijuana use does not seem to lead to medical problems or dependency, what she would say to our college-age sons and daughters about why they shouldn't try it. The only thing she could come up with on the spot was "because it is illegal." Well, yes, that is true, but that did not stop at least half of us twenty or thirty years ago, and it probably won't stop college-age students today. But there are ample reasons to tell your tween and teenager that you hope they will not experiment with marijuana or other drugs and that there will be consequences if they do.

I called Dr. Barthwell after the reunion to discuss her reactions to the audience. She said that she was not surprised. In her experience, most baby-boomer and Gen X parents' information about marijuana is informed more by their own experience twenty and thirty years ago than by the science of what we know today. She said she thinks all parents should communicate a "no-use ever" policy, that the research is compelling that marijuana is most dangerous for the youngest teens, and that the earlier one begins, the higher the rates of potential abuse and negative outcomes. She urged parents to communicate the message that marijuana use is not safe, that its use is worth preventing, and that it is not an inevitable right of passage for teens.

WHAT AFFIRMING PARENTS CAN DO

Parenting style makes a difference in whether your child experiments with, uses, or abuses alcohol and drugs. There is no guarantee that your teen will never try drugs or alcohol, but your actions can reduce the chances. Research indicates that parents can help delay their children's experimentation with substances, as well as help them limit it to experimental use.

For example, children of Permissive and Neglectful Parents are more likely to drink and to begin drinking earlier. Studies show that, on average, children of Permissive Parents begin drinking one year earlier than children of Neglectful Parents and two years earlier than children of Authoritarian and Affirming Parents. Children of both Authoritarian and Affirming Parents are less likely to drink or do drugs, but only children of Affirming Parents have significantly lower rates of binge drinking in college. Children in homes where parents provide limits about alcohol use, who have agreed with their parents about the clear consequences for drinking, and who are monitored by their parents (such as no unchaperoned parties and insisting on waking up a parent when they get home from a night out) drink less or do not drink at all. Monitoring seems especially to reduce alcohol use in boys. Affirming Parents can do a lot.

1. Stay involved in your teens' lives.

Staying involved in your teens' lives makes a difference in drinking and drugs, just as it does with sex and other high-risk behaviors. Knowing where they are after school, knowing their friends, setting limits on their behaviors, outlining consequences and then sticking to them all result in teens who are less likely to use alcohol and drugs. Teens, both younger and older, who report a high sense of connection to their parents are much less likely to drink or use marijuana.

Good communication, high emotional warmth, and even physical affection between parent and child lower the risk of alcohol and drug use. In some studies, parents' high expectations for academic performance also lead to lower drinking and other substance use—although too much pressure is likely to backfire, as young people turn to substances to mediate their stress.

2. Assure your child's safety.

Affirming Parents also want to assure our children's safety, despite our not wanting them to drink alcohol outside our homes or ever do drugs. It is imperative that your children know they can turn to you for a ride when they or the friend who drove them have been drinking, but they also need to hear repeatedly your expectation that they will not drink at all away from home. It is similar to the message we want to give our children about sexual intercourse and drugs: we don't want you to do it, but if you do, we don't want you to get hurt, so be safe. I hate that almost a third of young people say that in the preceding thirty days they had ridden with a driver who had been drinking alcohol. That's down from 1991, when 40 percent of young people answered yes to that question, but it's still way too high and too dangerous. One of the few absolute rules I suggest setting with your tween and teen should be that they are never, ever to get in a car with a driver who has been drinking or using drugs.

But you need to give them concrete options for how to get home if they find themselves faced with that situation: for example, "Call me, I will pick you up"; "Here's the number for Safe Rides— use it even if you're not sure you have to." But you also need to set a real and meaningful consequence for what you will do if you find out that they have been in a car with a driver who has been drinking. A month without driving privileges for a sixteen- or seventeen-year-old, no rides with friends for a fifteen-year-old, or not going anyplace they can't walk to might all be good deterrents.

3. Set consequences.

Whether teenagers believe that their parents will impose serious consequences if they find out they have been drinking or using marijuana makes a dramatic difference in whether teens drink or use drugs. Affluent teens know that their parents will be upset if they are rude to significant adults or do poorly at school, but a majority said that they do not think their parents would mind if they used alcohol. In studies, teenagers who do not anticipate parental consequences from their drinking were more likely to drink than teenagers who did. Two-thirds of teens say that losing their parents' respect and pride is one of the main reasons they do not smoke marijuana or use other drugs.

What might be the consequences of finding out that your young teen has been drinking? Well, this is an easy place to apply the "natural consequences" I spoke of earlier. For example:

- If I find out that you've been drinking and then driving, you lose car privileges for a specified amount of time.
- If you are thirteen and I find out that you have been drinking with a friend after school, you can't be in the house with a friend unless an adult is there, and you will need to be in a supervised after-care program.
- If you are sent home from camp or a program because you are found to be drinking, you will pay us back for the program, however long it takes.

• If you are hungover on a Sunday morning, you will still go to church with us.

Discussing the consequences in advance with your child is the key. The teenager who thinks, "I will just get in too much trouble if I drink," is much less likely to do so, especially if you involve him or her in setting the consequences in advance. Helping your teenager make good decisions about alcohol use also helps him or her make healthy decisions about other drugs.

4. Limit access.

Easy access to alcohol contributes to teenage drinking. Two out of three teens in a national study said that getting alcohol from home without their parents' knowledge would be easy. Think for a minute: How easy would it be for your tween to pour a drink in your home without your permission if you were not at home? When I asked that recently at a parent education session, every parent in the room admitted it would be very easy. They had unlocked liquor cabinets, and beer bottles and open bottles of wine in their refrigerators. Unless there is alcoholism in the family, we need to teach our teens moderation and responsible drinking. How? Dr. Hanson explains that the adults need to model healthy behaviors in their own alcohol use. What about allowing your preteen or young teenager to have sips of your own drinks? Dr. Hanson suggests that you know the law in your state. In some states, it is illegal for parents to give alcohol to their own minor children. We have allowed our children to taste our wine or beer from the first time they asked; it seemed better to satisfy their curiosity than deny it.

5. Be clear on your rules.

A clear, unambiguous no-alcohol rule (beyond a few sips at a family dinner) should continue until children are at least fifteen or sixteen. There is convincing data that people who begin drinking in childhood are much more likely to have problems with alcohol in adolescence and adulthood. There is also some research showing that alcohol use in adolescent rats is more likely to affect learning and memory than alcohol use in adult rats. (The researchers use rats because they can't ethically or legally give a randomly selected group of underage teens alcohol and then test their responses.) As discussed in chapter 5, the brain is undergoing rapid development during these early adolescent years, and alcohol and other drug use can affect that development.

6. Know your child's friends.

Young people who have friends who drink or use drugs also drink and use drugs. Even if they just think that their friends or even their peers are drinking or using drugs, they're more likely to use. Countless parents have told me that although their children are hanging out with a tough crowd, they know their children would not engage in these behaviors themselves. That's not likely. If you think their friends are using, they probably are too. Talk to them.

7. Know the signs of drinking or drug use.

It may be easier to know whether your children have been drinking than whether they have been using drugs. Many of the signs of drug use are easy to confuse with the normal emotional ups and downs of the early adolescent years, and some can be signs of physical or mental illness. Talking to a health professional if your child exhibits these characteristics will be helpful in making an assessment.

Here's a list I have adapted from Partnership for a Drug-Free America (www.drugfree.org). They suggest that you look for:

- Teens who are *unusually* withdrawn, depressed, tired, hostile, and uncooperative.
- Teenagers who begin to be *unusually* careless about their grooming.
- Deteriorating relationships with family members and old friends. A sudden new group of friends who appear to be involved with drugs is a very good sign that your child has begun using.
- A sudden drop in grades and interest in hobbies, sports, and other activities they used to enjoy. Finding out that your

child is skipping school or missing other activities begs you to ask where they have been and what they were doing.

Some of the signs that the Partnership for a Drug-Free America mentions are too obvious to be missed:

- If your child is stealing from you.
- If your child does not have a cold but has a runny nose and red-rimmed eyes.
- If your child can't hold a coherent discussion with you after time away from home or time alone in their room.
- If your prescription bottles for tranquilizers, pain medication, and sleeping aids are suddenly depleted. (In fact, if you use such medications and have a tween or teen in your house, I suggest limiting your child's access to them. Put them away in a locked place. Know how many pills are in the bottle. Remember, access makes a difference.)
- Drug paraphernalia: rolling papers, pipes, bongs. And don't accept the perennial teenage explanation that they are just holding them for a friend.

I'll discuss the issues related to snooping or spying on your child in greater depth in chapter 9, but suspecting drug use is the only reason that I think gives us license to invade our tweens' and teenagers' privacy. I have told both of my children that I would never read their mail or their journals, or open drawers and closets in their rooms, unless I was concerned that they were using illegal substances. Then all bets would be off. And although I do not support random drug testing of children and teens, if your child has been a drug user in the past, routine testing is something to consider with a treatment provider as well.

Of course, all these guidelines may be more difficult to implement for those of us who experimented with drugs when we were young, and most of us were able to drink legally at the age of eighteen. This leads to one more challenge that our parents didn't have to face.

"Mom and Dad, How Old Were You?"

Most likely our own parents didn't have to deal with this issue. But today's parents dread the day when their child asks: "Mom, how old were you when you first had sex?" "Dad, did you ever smoke marijuana?" "Did you drink in high school?" I remember once reading an Ellen Goodman column in the *Boston Globe* where she wrote something like, Baby boomers did everything. Regret nothing. And want their children to do none of it.

How do you handle these questions? Well, the first thing to do is be prepared for them and think through the values you want to convey to your children. What messages do you want to give them about their involvement with sex, alcohol, cigarettes, and other substance use? Do you hope that they will abstain now? Through high school? Forever? What values and expectations do you want to communicate to your child, and will they change as they get older?

You next need to think through whether your own history is likely to support or undermine those values. I was the ultimate "good girl" in high school, so my own answer to most of these questions as Alyssa and now Greg asks them is, "When I was in college." Both my professional understanding about adolescent brain development and my personal hopes and values that they will have the skills and maturity of late adolescence before they make these decisions in their lives lead me to hope that my children will wait until college as well.

But what if you began regular drinking, sex, or drug use at a young age but hope that your children will wait much longer? Parents have two options in this situation. We can look at the larger issue behind our children's questions about our personal histories. Yes, they are curious about what we have done, but more likely they are wondering how they will know if *they* are ready to make these decisions.

I do not believe that you owe your child full disclosure about your sexual or substance history. If the age you first engaged in one of these behaviors is younger than you would like for your child, you can answer something like, "Honey, I am not comfortable sharing with you some of these very personal parts of my life. But it sounds like you are thinking about how people know if they are ready for sex (alcohol, cigarettes, and so on), and that is something I am happy to discuss with you. Is there an age when you think most people are ready?"

Or you can choose to share your history and then explain why you don't want your child to repeat it: "Honey, I first drank when I was in the eighth grade, and I remember getting drunk in the ninth. But, looking back, I think that was a pretty dumb move on my part because I got caught, lost my parents' trust for a while, and lost privileges. I also took some dumb risks with my health. Today we know that early drinking can hurt teens' developing brains."

Whichever strategy you take, the goal is to turn this into a dialogue, not a lecture. I have a sign in my office that says, "What people need is a good listening to." That is, as opposed to a "good talking to," and it includes children and adolescents. We want to seek the middle ground of the Affirming Parent: share our values, jointly set limits, identify the consequences and stick to them, and love and nurture our children. We also want to help them practice how they will respond to peer pressure.

Sex, alcohol, and drug use were all big issues when we were teenagers. But we face new challenges for our children today. Let's turn to two of parents' greatest fears—abductions and sexual abuse—in the next chapter.

TEST YOUR FEAR FACTOR

1. The number of child abductions compared to 1988 is:
   a. Increasing.
   b. Decreasing.
   c. Staying the same.

2. The incidence of child sexual abuse compared to 1992 is:
   a. Increasing.
   b. Decreasing.
   c. Staying the same.

3. Children and teens are most likely to be abducted by someone they met:
   a. On the Internet.
   b. On the street.
   c. At a shopping mall.
   d. In their home.

4. A girl child is most likely to be sexually abused by:
   a. A stranger.
   b. A relative.
   c. A teenager.
   d. A family friend.

5. A boy child is most likely to be sexually abused by:
   a. A stranger.
   b. A relative.
   c. A teenager.
   d. A family friend.

* * * * *

Answers: 1. b; 2. b; 3. d; 4. b; 5. c.

CHAPTER 8

The Truth About Abductions and Sexual Abuse

REMEMBER GOING out to play? I grew up in a large suburb in the 1960s. Every Saturday morning during the school year and every day in the summer, I would leave the house right after breakfast and not come home until lunchtime. If you were like me, you did not have "play dates" arranged and accompanied by parents; you just went out into the fields or woods or parks near your home and looked for other kids to play with. When you came home, no one asked where you had been. It was assumed you'd been "out playing."

Recently, at a training workshop at our congregation for new teacher volunteers in our religious education program, we asked participants for their earliest memories of their spirituality. One after another, people talked about experiences in nature as a child, mostly without an adult present. They recounted going into the woods with friends, discovering a brook or a stream, sleeping out at night under the stars for the first time, or just getting on a bicycle and riding aimlessly for miles.

When I asked how many of the parents allowed their children the same freedom they had enjoyed to explore nature and the outdoors on their own, only one of them raised a hand.

Many parents believe that the world is a more dangerous place than when we were small. There is a sense that there are more child kidnappings, more sexual abuse, and more school violence. As parents, we are hesitant to allow our children to walk to school alone, much less go out to play without a destination, an organized play date, or a parent, nanny, or much older sibling to accompany them. Ironically, though, many of us let our children hang out in cyberspace without guidance and think nothing of dropping our tweens or young teens off at a mall or multiplex to meet their friends inside.

Hundreds of companies have as their slogan some variation of "Safety is job number one." That's true for most parents as well. When our children are small, we put away the cleaning supplies, cover the wall sockets, install gates at the head of the stairs, and (I hope) buckle our children into infant seats and booster seats. (A surprisingly high number of parents—one-quarter—fail to insist on car seats for their children ages four to seven, but three-quarters do take this important step to keep their children safe.) Affirming Parents of small children do all they can to control the environment to keep their children safe. But as our children grow up and move out in the world, how can we keep them safe while allowing them more freedom?

In this chapter, we will look at child kidnappings and child sexual abuse, two of the biggest concerns for parents. In the next chapter, I'll discuss Internet safety, especially the new social networking sites.

FACT vs. FEAR

Our children are no more likely to be abused or kidnapped than we were as children in the 1960s, 1970s, and early 1980s. School violence is going down, not up. According to the U.S. Centers for Disease Control and Prevention, fewer young people are carrying weapons, fewer children are in physical fights, and school shootings, despite how horrific they are when they occur, are episodic and very rare. According to Dr. Jonathan Fast, professor of social work at Yeshiva University and an expert on school violence, "Schools are the safest place your child can be. Crime in school usually involves items stolen from an unlocked locker. Most injuries happen in gym."

It may be comforting to know that you don't need to worry much about your children while they're at school, but what about their risk from strangers?

"Stranger Danger"

My friend and colleague Dr. Kate Ott lets her four-year-old daughter watch a television show on public broadcasting most mornings for a few minutes as they are getting ready to leave their home. They often see a public service ad warning children not to let strangers talk to them or touch them. Her daughter asks, looking for reassurance about the family who takes care of her, "Mama, the Smiths are not strangers, right? So nothing can happen to me there?" And Kate reassures her daughter often that, yes, she is safe, but that if anyone, even someone she knows and likes, ever touches her in a way that makes her uncomfortable, she must tell her mom. Kate worries that the stranger danger message is going to leave her child vulnerable to abuse by someone she knows well.

Our children are being taught to be fearful of strangers. There are 276,000 sites on Google that use the term *stranger danger* and dozens of books for children with *stranger danger* in the title.

You may have had a similar experience to the following: A charming three-year-old girl is in front of me in a cart in a checkout line at the supermarket. I smile at her and say, "Hi." She begins to shriek, reaching out to her mother to be picked up. She looks terrified. "Mommy, Mommy," she wails, "that stranger is *talking* to me." I apologize quickly to the mother, who glares at me.

Whenever something like this happens, I think to myself, What message has this child received about the world? Not to trust anyone? How will this fear affect her as she begins to move into the world on her own? Might those messages about strangers feed into social anxiety as she grows up? Do you remember the story about the Boy Scout who was lost in the woods in Utah who would not come out when he heard his name called because he had been taught never to go with strangers?

I understand that the fear of a stranger abducting our child is every parent's nightmare. We have all heard about the tragedies that befell Elizabeth Smart, Megan Kanka (for whom Megan's Law is named), Polly Klaas, Amber Hagerman (for whom Amber Alerts are named), and Adam Walsh (for whom a new federal law is named).

Our hearts go out to their families, and these crimes have affected how the nation approaches these issues. These horrible and gut-wrenching stories stay with us—but they also misguide us.

It seems that almost every week we hear about a child or young teenager being abducted. States have instituted programs called Amber Alerts, named after nine-year-old Amber Hagerman, who was kidnapped while out for a ride on her bicycle and murdered in Texas. When an Amber Alert is posted, the Emergency Alert System, set up for weather emergencies, broadcasts a bulletin on television and radio stations to report that a child is missing. When I hear one, my heart always stops a bit.

But are there more abductions today than when we were children? Is it more dangerous to allow your child to ride a bike to school than when we were growing up? What about all those pictures of children on the milk cartons and flyers asking, *Have You Seen Me?*

Despite the increase in media attention, the number of serious child kidnappings may actually have *decreased* slightly since the late 1980s. The Department of Justice (DOJ) estimated that there were 200 to 300 cases of child kidnappings by strangers in 1988; today they estimate between 60 and 170 children a year. There is some question whether the decrease is a result of changes in reporting requirements, but the DOJ states that abductions "do not appear to be any more frequent...than in 1988."

Were you surprised to learn that only 60 to 170 children are kidnapped each year? I was. The number that stuck in my head from popular media reports is that nearly a million children are reported missing each year. That number is true, but fewer than 2 percent of them are abducted by nonfamily members. And even among nonfamily members, a majority of the perpetrators are well known to the child, with 1 in 10 being an authority figure or a care provider. Even more reassuringly, according to the U.S. Department of Justice report, 99.8 percent of reported missing children are returned home or located in a very short period of time. That's right: *99.8 percent.*

Almost 9 in 10 children who are reported missing have run away from home (runaways account for 45 percent of missing cases), been thrown out of their homes, or are the result of what

DOJ calls "benign circumstances," such as a miscommunication or misunderstanding about the child's whereabouts. (I remember one frightening hour when Alyssa was in the seventh grade when I thought she was coming home, and she had forgotten to tell us that she had an additional band practice.) Although many people assume that missing children are taken by family members related to custody disputes, those account for fewer than 1 in 13 cases.

The image most of us have when we think about missing children is children under the age of twelve, maybe even under the age of eight. Wrong again. Teenagers are by far the most frequent victims. Seventy-seven percent of all reported missing children are teenagers, 81 percent of all nonfamily abductions involve teenagers, and 58 percent of all kidnappings happen to adolescents. Many times, the teens reported missing are with their romantic partners or ex-romantic partners, sometimes not voluntarily. Many have run away from home, often because of abuse or harassment, or because they are gay, lesbian, or transgender and have been told by their angry parents never to come home again. The Web site of the National Center for Missing and Exploited Children recently showed a photo of an androgynous seventeen-year-old with a girl's name. The note said she had been missing for a few days, and that she would only answer to the name "Max." My heart went out to what I guessed was a transgender teen who had left home rather than face her parents' disapproval of her gender identity.

For the hundred or so families a year whose young child is the victim of a stranger abduction—in just under half of these cases, the child is killed or never recovered—the pain is beyond our understanding. But the media images of the small child preyed upon by strangers is, thankfully, not what the vast majority of parents need to stay up nights worrying about.

Please understand that I am not saying that it is not important to talk to our children about how to protect themselves from people they don't know who might want to do them harm. It is common sense to teach your children and teens that, in the words of the Center for Missing and Exploited Children, they "should always check first with you [the parent] or a trusted adult before they go anywhere, accept anything, or get into a car with anyone." They also encourage you to have a yearly updated good-quality digitized photo of your child, just in case it needs to be disseminated fast. The Center wants parents to know that if your child or teenager goes missing, you should immediately call your local law enforcement agency and then call their hotline at 1-800-THE-LOST.

Parents should definitely rehearse with their children and even teenagers what to do if they get separated from you in a store or out-side venue. You may have seen the pieces on network television shows like *Dateline* and *Today* suggesting that our children can be easily persuaded to help adults who claim that they have lost their dogs or that they need directions. I did not believe that my son would fall for such ruses. When he was in the sixth grade, I asked him what he would do if someone he didn't know came to school to pick him up, saying there'd been an emergency and that I'd asked him to drive Greg to the hospital to meet me. He thought for a moment. "Well, I would ask to use their cell phone to call you to check that you had sent them," he reasoned. Wrong answer. The person would then have had him close enough to pull him into the car and drive off.

I explained that I would *never, ever* send someone he didn't know to pick him up. In a real emergency, I would call the school and tell them that either one of our relatives or a close friend would be picking him up. I realized that we needed to rehearse this situation again in a few days. It's not that Greg wasn't thinking; it's that he was using the concrete thinking of a twelve-year-old child. I needed to be equally concrete in preparing him for this situation.

I do worry that by emphasizing the risk of strangers, we are not empowering children to protect themselves the way they need to in the world. I also wonder about the cost to children who grow up fearful of people they don't know or with the idea that they always have to be on guard. We want our children to be safe and discerning about situations that might put them at risk, but we also want them to feel safe and trusting in the world. I do not want my children growing up with the sense that the world and its people are danger-ous and out to get them—and I want them to play outside and feel safe in nature.

I confess that this grows out of a personal place for me. My parents grew up in the United States at the time of the Holocaust. My grandparents, first-generation American Jews, survived when other members of the family were murdered in Europe. The world *was* a dangerous place for Jews in the mid-twentieth century. The threat of the Holocaust and the cold war was communicated to me as a child as a generalized insecurity and lack of trust in the physical world. I was somewhat accident-prone as a child, and to this day, as I tackle new physical adventures, I hear my mother's voice in the back of my head saying, "Don't do that; you might hurt yourself." She was always offering threats of impending doom around the corner: "Go outside barefoot and your feet will be cut to shreds" or "You'll catch pneumonia if you go outside with a wet head." Her desire to protect me and my sister was real and intense, and it still affects me today.

Let's move on to the second major concern many parents have about their children's safety.

FACING THE REALITIES OF SEXUAL ABUSE

Childhood and teenage sexual abuse is a pervasive and devastating public health issue. Half a million children and youth are thought to be sexually abused each year. According to a number of studies, 17–25 percent of women and 10–15 percent of men report having been sexually abused before the age of eighteen. The repercussions of childhood sexual abuse are often lifelong: adults who were sexually abused as children are more likely to be depressed and to have problems with intimacy and sexuality in their adult relationships. Keeping children safe from sexual abuse must become a far greater national and parental priority.

The common image of a sex offender is a strange-looking middle-aged man lurking around a playground, eyeing potential victims. His contemporary counterpart hangs around a computer chat room, hoping to entice your child to meet him someplace to have sex. The *actual* profile of the person most likely to offend is someone well known to the child, someone who may also be a teenager, and—high-profile cases like former Congressman Mark Foley's to the contrary—for boys, more likely to be a teenage female than an adult male.

In 9 out of 10 cases, children know their sexual abusers well. They are parents, family members, neighbors, clergy, coaches, and teachers. Family friends and relatives are the primary offenders; family friends are more likely to offend with boys, and relatives to offend with girls. One in seven abused girls is abused by a father, stepfather, or boyfriend of her mother, although only 3 percent of boys are abused by people in these categories. But teenagers are much more likely to be abused by a family member: one-quarter of offenders of victims' ages twelve through seventeen are related to them.

Girls are sexually abused primarily by men, while boys are abused by both men and women. In 70 percent of the cases of sexual abuse of boys, the perpetrator is an adolescent, often a babysitter or an older family friend. According to Stop It Now, an organization that works to prevent child sexual abuse, half of childhood sexual abuse is committed by children and youth against other, less powerful children. And despite high-profile media cases of sexual abuse against children in churches and schools, nearly 5 out of every 6 sexual assaults against children occur in someone's home, not a public place.

In other words, just as with missing children, instilling a fear of strangers in our children will not keep them safe from sexual abuse. All the "stranger danger" protection messages in the world will not give your child the skills to know what to do when Uncle Joe or your best friend or a babysitter starts to groom him or her for a "special relationship" that includes sexual contact.

Because of the increased amount of time children spend today with adults other than their parents—nannies, babysitters, athletic coaches, caregivers in after-school programs—we face the need to trust other adults with our children in a way unknown to previous generations of parents. It is critical for you to make sure that schools, religious institutions, leagues, and community agencies screen their workers for histories of sexual offenses.

The good news is that the incidence of child sexual abuse cases may actually be *declining*. A 2002 report for the Department of Justice found that "sexual abuse cases substantiated by child protective services dropped a remarkable 39% between 1992 and 1999."

They believe that the reason for the decline is most likely prevention efforts, improved treatment methods for sex offenders, and more aggressive prosecution of offenders. We are now also talking more about sexual-abuse prevention, prevention efforts are more common in elementary schools, and we have recognized that preventing child sexual abuse must be a community priority.

WHAT AFFIRMING PARENTS CAN DO

So, how do we keep our children safe and yet give them a sense of trust in the world? Dr. Laurence Steinberg, a psychologist at Temple University, says it well in his book *The Ten Basic Principles of Good Parenting*: "Protect when you must. Permit when you can."

1. Teach our children that the world is a wonderful place and that the vast majority of adults would never hurt children.

When you hear or see an Amber Alert while in the car with your children, reassure them that in almost all cases, children are not taken by strangers but by family members. Remind them how you hope they will behave if someone they don't know well asks them to go with them. If you're divorced or separated, remind them of your agreements with the other parent about custody or visiting.

It's also very important to reassure your child when there is a high-profile case of child abduction or a sexual offender in your neighborhood in the news. I remember my daughter being terrified at twelve by the news reports of young Polly Klaas being abducted from her bedroom. I also remember putting two batons under my bed when I was about that age to protect myself from the Boston Strangler, whom I fantasized making his way down to my bedroom in Connecticut. Talking to your children about these media stories allows you to address their fears, which can quickly grow out of proportion.

2. Practice with your children what to do if an adult approaches them in an inappropriate way.

Begin by reminding your children that most adults would never hurt a child, but that it is always unsafe to go off somewhere with any adult without your explicit permission. Talk calmly with your children, tweens, and, yes, adolescents about how to stay safe, reassuring them that they will know what to do if a situation becomes threatening. They need to know that you will believe them, and that they should always tell you if something odd happens during their day. If they witness something that makes them uncomfortable, they should tell you. Let them know that adults do not try to become friends with children they don't know, and that they should tell you if an adult is becoming overly friendly in a way that does not seem right. Help them understand that adults do not need to ask children for directions, for help in finding a dog, and so on, and that if a grownup asks them to keep a secret, to tell you anyway. The National Center for Missing and Exploited Children suggests teaching children that it is "more important to get out of a threatening situation than to be polite." Your children need to learn to handle phone calls when you're not home: they can screen them using the answering machine and let people leave messages, or say that Mom or Dad is in the shower, for example.

Many of these same suggestions will help children avoid sexual abuse as well, which is the motive in a considerable number of child abductions.

3. Teach your child to "tell."

Research tells us that most children and teens do not tell anyone when they've been sexually abused. Few teenagers who have been victims of an attempted date rape tell their parents, and even fewer tell their parents about inappropriate materials they find on the Internet.

If your child is small, you want to be able to recognize the signs of possible child sexual abuse. They include an unusual discharge from the penis or the vagina and a child who draws genitals in pictures, fondles a pet or stuffed animal in sexual ways, or consistently rubs or touches his or her genitals in public, even after being asked to do it in private. You need to understand that while sex play between children of similar ages is often healthy curiosity, sex play between children more than three years apart in age is most often problematic and may be abusive. It is usual for children up until about the third grade to play doctor or "you show me yours, I'll show you mine," but any type of penetration, whether with fingers, objects, or penises, could be cause for concern.

4. Make sure your child is informed.

The best defense is giving your children the skills to recognize when an adult is acting inappropriately with them, as well as a sense of what to do if an adult tries to engage them in inappropriate behavior. Even small children must know the names of all the parts of the body, including their genitals, and they must trust that adults will believe them if they "tell on" another adult. Children who learn that their bodies are good and that their sexuality is a gift know how to make good decisions and have the language to communicate accurately and effectively about sexuality. They are also being prepared to respond appropriately if faced with abusive behaviors, to assert their right to control their own bodies, and to tell a trusted adult if such behaviors occur.

Children who understand that their bodies belong to them and that no one else should touch them anywhere without their consent are less likely to be vulnerable to an adult offender. Every child, from the age of three through high school, can learn "No, Go, Tell": say no to the abuse; leave the situation immediately, or as soon as possible; and tell a parent or caregiver if someone tries to hurt them or asks them to keep a secret about touching.

5. Screen child-care workers and babysitters.

Always screen child-care workers and babysitters for histories of sex offenses, and ask whether sponsoring agencies do routine screening and background checks on day-care and nursery-school caregivers, coaches, Scout leaders, after-school workers, religious educators, and so on. People who are sexually attracted to children often try to work or volunteer with children and begin their relationships in these seemingly innocuous situations; parents banding together to insist on screening and background checks helps keep our children safe. This may be harder than warning your children about strangers, but it's important.

It's also important to speak with nannies and babysitters about whether they were sexually abused as children and, if they were, whether they have been in therapy for these issues. Although most people who were sexually abused do not go on to become offenders themselves, some do. So it's important to get your own child professional help if this happens.

6. Understand that sex offender registries will not keep your children safe.

As you may know, every state is now required to keep a computerized list of registered sex offenders, and you can search online to find out if any live in your neighborhood. I have a lot of reservations about these registries. Despite pronouncements that such laws protect our children, I doubt that they keep children safe. Remember that the person most likely to abuse your child is someone he or she is close to—a family member, family friend, even a nanny or baby-sitter—who has never been convicted. People end up on sex offender registry lists for many reasons, including older teens who had consensual sex with underage partners. There have been several vigilante-style murders of people on these lists, not very different from the lynchings of the twentieth century. Many of the people on these registries have served time in prison and are unlikely to commit such crimes again, especially those who have completed treatment programs. (The Department of Justice, in a review of sixty-one published studies, found that only 13 percent of people who had sexually molested children had a repeat offense.)

Civil rights and moral issues aside, I'm also concerned that sex offender registries may give parents a false sense of security. I've learned of several communities that require registered sex offenders to spend Halloween evening at the local community center. But this action was not coupled with any prevention messages to parents. Surely we do not want our children, tweens, or teens going into anyone's home alone while trick-or-treating. Just because the person down the street is not on a registry does not mean it is safe for your child to come inside that person's house. How much safer children might have been if these communities had developed parent-child education programs that teach parents that they should accompany children who are trick-or-treating, that older youth need to go in groups, that trick-or-treating should take place at the front door, and under no circumstances should children or teens enter anyone's home.

I recently read about a new tracking system that preys on parents' fears about convicted sex offenders. By installing this system on your child's cell phone and then linking it to your cell phone's text messaging system, for $19.95 a month you can receive an instant message that lets you know when your child spends more than one minute in an area where a registered sex offender lives or works. Picture yourself in a meeting or at a luncheon, and your cell phone beeps with a notice that your nine-year-old is in the vicinity of a building where a known sex offender lives or works. Depending on where your child walks or bike-rides, you could receive several such messages a day! Not only would I not want to handle that type of ongoing anxiety, but such a system is not going to keep children safe from the people most likely to abuse them: not treated sex offenders, but people they know well in their daily lives.

In the next chapter, I'll discuss perhaps the biggest change in our parenting challenges: the rapidly increasing role that computers and other technologies play in the lives of our children, tweens, and teens.

TEST YOUR FEAR FACTOR

1. Heavy TV viewing among young people is:
   a. Increasing.
   b. Decreasing.
   c. Staying about the same.

2. Compared to ten years ago, young people spend:
   a. More hours with media each day.
   b. Fewer hours with media each day.
   c. About the same number of hours with media each day.

3. The percentage of teenagers who have been solicited online for sex is:
   a. 75%.
   b. 50%.
   c. 15%.

4. Teenagers are most likely to be bullied:
   a. On the school bus.
   b. At school.
   c. Online.

5. Compared to five years ago, child and teen Internet use is:
   a. Increasing.
   b. Decreasing.
   c. Staying the same.

* * * * *

Answers: 1. b; 2. c; 3. c; 4. b; 5. a.

CHAPTER 9

Couch Potato, Mouse Potato: Navigating the New Electronic World

YOUNG PEOPLE today are surrounded by media. According to a study by the Kaiser Family Foundation, the typical home with children now has "3.6 CD or tape players, 3.5 televisions, 2.9 VCR/DVD players, 2.1 video game consoles, and 1.5 computers." One in four children lives in a home with five or more television sets. How does your home compare? These numbers are about right for our home, but mostly because we never seem to get rid of the old items once they've been replaced. Right now, we have two television sets in the attic that don't work, two outdated computers, and a nonfunctioning Nintendo. Oh yes, there is also a record turntable somewhere.

VCRs, DVDs, video game consoles, MP3 players, flat-screen TVs, and personal computers were not invented when you were growing up. The new media that surround our children today create a new landscape for parenting. It can be overwhelming to sort out what parts of this new landscape are beneficial to our children and what parts, if any, we should worry about, including whether our children are spending too much time "plugged in."

FACT vs. FEAR

It sometimes feels as though our children are constantly using some type of electronic device. Though research shows that the amount of time young people spend with media overall has actually remained the same since 1999, according to the Kaiser Family Foundation study, "there have been numerous incremental changes that added together have substantially expanded the presence of media in young people's lives." For example, MP3 players and iPods did not exist in 1999, and there was no TiVo. More homes now have high-speed Internet access, more homes have cable or satellite TV, and instant messaging and private Web pages have emerged. But the fact that the total amount of time spent on media has not changed since 1999 indicates that young people, in the words of the Kaiser report, "may have hit a ceiling in terms of the portion of their day they can devote to media."

It may surprise you that most children and teens still spend more time watching television and listening to music than using the computer. A whopping 8 in 10 young people watch television on most days, compared with just under half who say they go online and a third who say they read a newspaper most days. But television viewing time is actually going down. Although 43 percent of teens watched for three or more hours a day in 1999, just 37 percent watched for three or more hours a day in 2005. Nevertheless, young people aged eight to eighteen consume nearly six and half hours of media each day. The average teen and child watches an average of three hours of television per day, and a total of nearly four hours a day with media, when time spent watching videos, DVDs, and TiVo'd programs is added. They spend about one and three-quarter hours a day listening to music on radios, CDs, or MP3 players. In comparison, on average, these young people spend about an hour a day on the computer and a little less than an hour playing video games. If these numbers sound like they add up to more than six, that's because they do: young people "multitask" their media. For a quarter of the time that young people use media, they're using more than one at a time, for instance, watching television or listening to music while surfing the Internet.

Most of the time they spend on the Internet is pretty productive: 94 percent use it to assist with homework; 89 percent send e-mails; 81 percent play games; 80 percent download music; 76 percent check the news. A third look for health information, and a quarter search for religious or spiritual guidance. More than half have talked to a parent about information they have found online.

But, despite scary media reports, heavy use of media does not seem to have a negative effect on most young people. According to the Kaiser Family Foundation, "those young people who spend the most time using media are also those whose lives are the most full with family, friends, sports, and other interests." Almost every report on childhood obesity points to increased television, computer, and video game time as part of the problem, but in this study, at least, both the light and heavy media users spent the same amount of time doing physical activity. Heavy television watchers spend the most time with their parents, although it's possible that is shared TV time. Heavy TV users actually spend a little *more* time in physical activity than their peers, and slightly more time doing chores and pursuing hobbies. And watching a lot of TV does not seem to affect their ability to concentrate on other tasks. A recent study of five thousand American kindergartners, published in *Pediatrics* in 2006, found that "children who watched the most television were no more likely to develop attention problems than those who watched the least television." Another study in the Netherlands came to the same conclusion.

21st-CENTURY CHALLENGES

As mentioned earlier, much of the media that our children spend time with today is new to us. But there are new aspects to one old technology that present new challenges for parents. So I will tackle TV first before moving on to the newer technologies.

Television

Of course, we had television when we were kids, and it has been a staple of young people's lives ever since. What has changed is the ubiquity of television, as well as its content. We had one TV in our home while I was growing up and five channels to watch. How many televisions did you have in the home you grew up in, and what do you remember watching?

Today, two-thirds of children and youth have a television set in their bedrooms. Two-thirds of young people say that the TV is usually on during meals, and half live in homes where the TV is left on most of the time. Despite the concerns parents express about the content of television programs, over half of children aged eight to eighteen said that there are *no* rules about television watching in their homes. In homes that do have media limits, only 1 in 5 children says that such limits are enforced regularly. In other words, parents look the other way. (I have to admit I am guilty; Greg is supposed to watch only two hours of television a day, but often watches more. He points out, though, that I often watch more than three, if you include the news!)

The Kaiser Family Foundation concluded that despite a generalized concern about young people's media use, when it comes to their own children, "the vast majority of parents either do not feel their children are spending too much time with media or have simply given up." Parents do not set time limits, they do not check parent advisories, they do not use parental controls, they leave the TV on at mealtimes, and they leave their children with unsupervised media use in their bedrooms. Many of us have no idea how to set the V-chip embedded in our TV sets.

The other huge difference from our childhoods is that the screen is now filled with sexual and violent content. According to the Kaiser Family Foundation, on average, there are five scenes that involve sex per hour on nightly television, up from 3.2 per hour in 1997–98. Seventy percent of all TV shows now contain some sexual content, compared with 56 percent in 1998.

The most common rule parents have is that homework or chores need to be done before TV watching. But only slightly more than 1 in 10 parents have rules about how *much* TV their children can watch or *which* TV shows children can watch, although 4 in 10 young people say that their parents generally know what they are watching on TV. Even fewer have explicit rules for Internet, iPod, or video game use. But more should.

Despite parents' general reluctance to monitor television use, at least we understand how TV and TV programs work. Let's move on to what may be parents' newest concern.

The Internet

Perhaps more than any other area I have discussed in this book, Internet access has changed our children's lives (and our lives as well) and challenged us as parents in different ways than other generations of parents. Access to the Internet in our homes has exploded; today almost three-quarters of homes in the United States have a computer with Internet access, compared with fewer than half just seven years ago.

According to the Kaiser Family Foundation study of media use among people ages eight to eighteen, 74 percent of children live in homes with Internet access, 31 percent have a computer in their bedroom, and 20 percent have Internet access in their bedrooms. Almost 9 in 10 (87 percent) of twelve- to seventeen-year-olds use the Internet, up from 75 percent in 2002. Sixty percent of sixth graders are online; that jumps to 82 percent in seventh and eighth grades, and a whopping 94 percent of all eleventh and twelfth graders. Half say they go online every day. A third send IMs every day. In 1990, a majority of teens said they did not think they could live without their radio or CD player. In 2004, it was their computer.

SEXUAL CONTENT

As I am writing this chapter, the story of ex-Congressman Mark Foley is absorbing the nation's attention. He was found sending salacious e-mails and IMs to pages who worked for the House of Representatives and was forced to resign. But, amid all the media coverage of the Foley scandal, there was not much attention paid to how frequently today's children and teens are exposed to inappropriate materials on the Internet. One in 7 ten- to seventeen-year-olds say that they have received a sexual solicitation online; only 4 percent say that someone they met on the Internet has invited them to meet them offline for sex. Now, reversing those statistics should give us some comfort: 6 in 7 young people have not been solicited, and 96 percent have not been asked to meet anyone offline. However, *70 percent* of teens say that they've come across sexually explicit materials accidentally while Web searching, and 1 in 3 reports having had an unwanted exposure to sexual material, up from 1 in 4 in 1999.

(To reassure you a bit, only 9 percent of young people report such exposure as upsetting; mostly they just click off.)

Any person with an e-mail address, including your child, is likely to receive spam messages that include sexual content. I was speaking at a suburban New York high school recently and learned how ubiquitous these messages are. During my talks on sexuality I always try to reassure teenage boys that "size does not matter" and that there isn't anything one can do, aside from an operation involving implants, to increase penis size. In every class I teach, one boy will raise his hand and say something like, "That's not true. Every day I get e-mail messages from people saying they can send me a medicine that makes penises larger." I tell them that these are scams, but sometimes they don't believe me. After all, they ask, if they don't work, why would people order them? Indeed. The Internet provides young people with a great deal of informal "sex education" even if they don't enter the world of searching, chat rooms, and social networking sites like MySpace.

SEXUAL SOLICITATION

Parents' biggest concerns about the Internet seem to be about online sexual solicitations. The good news is that only 1 in 7 young people has been solicited online (including other teens), and that is actually fewer than five years ago. Only 11 percent of young people report that they have formed a relationship with someone they met online, and that is down as well. And rather than the image most of us have of the middle-aged predator, reinforced by *Dateline* specials, most solicitations come from other teenagers or from adults under the age of twenty-five. In fact, when teenagers say they met someone offline, it is often a same-age friend of a friend.

CYBERBULLYING

The other concern the media tells us to worry about is online bullying. I have seen countless reports on morning and evening news shows about this "cyberbullying." In 2005, according to the Second Youth Internet Safety Survey, 1 in 11 youth said they had been harassed on the Internet; if we switch that statistic around, 10 in 11 young people have not been. Despite media headlines about Internet bullying, 85 percent of young people have not been harassed. In almost all cases of online harassment, it simply ended on its own or when the person logged off, left the site, or blocked future messages. Most harassment by online acquaintances involves a single interaction, not exactly the image of Internet bullying that the media covers.

But that is not to say it's not a problem for the 9 percent of young people who have been harassed this way, especially those few (1.5 to 3 percent) who say they receive harassing messages at least weekly. About 4 in 10 of these young people report feeling very or extremely upset or afraid because of the incidents. Most young people don't tell an adult about their harassment, whether it's online or in person. Two-thirds don't tell a parent; almost none tell a teacher. But most do tell a friend. So it may be going on without your knowledge.

Internet harassment, though new to us and thus perhaps more frightening, is far less frequent than harassment of other kinds. Fully 80 percent of high school students say they've been subjected to verbal harassment in the preceding year: this includes teasing and rumors and lies being spread about them. Forty percent say that they've been pushed, shoved, or tripped in the past year. For teenagers, it's probably safer to be online than in school.

SOCIAL NETWORKING SITES

Lately parents' fears about social networking sites have been garnering a lot of media attention. You have heard of MySpace and Facebook, but there are other, smaller sites such as tribe.net, xanga.com, sconex, bebo, tagged, and livejournal. And by the time you read this, I'm sure there will be other sites as well. People (not just teenagers and college students) use these sites to create their own Web pages, where they post photos, music, blogs, and other personal information.

MySpace is currently the biggest of the sites. Since its beginning in 1993, it has grown to more than 100 million users. Users are supposed to be at least fourteen years old, but in some middle schools, MySpace accounts are common. It's very popular across the country with high school students and young people who are not in college (college users usually are on Facebook.com).

These social networking sites actually have benefits, despite our concerns about them. They teach young people the art of networking and some pretty sophisticated computer skills. (Do you know how to add videos to *your* Web site?) They can be godsends to shy teens and to those, including gay or bisexual teens, who do not fit in at school. These accounts (which cost nothing) allow young people to share pictures, send mail and instant messages, and write blogs and comments.

Some of you are probably thinking that you can just skip this section because you won't give your child or teen permission to go on these sites. I certainly think you can limit your tweens' use of them—after all, MySpace itself does not allow users younger than fourteen. But forbidding your ninth-to-twelfth grader to have a page is not realistic in communities where most of the high school students have one. Social networking sites and the Internet are facts of life for today's teenagers, whether we like it or not. According to blogsafety.org: "pulling the plug on your child's Internet activities is rarely a good response to a problem—it is too easy for them to 'go underground' and establish free messaging and social networking accounts at a friend's house or many other places."

Marc Fernandes, a sexuality educator in New York, says that sites like MySpace are "pen-pal and chain letters on speed." The intimacy that can build up on the Internet sites can literally take minutes, not months or years. It can be quite eye-opening to go on MySpace. Anyone can browse—try it. You can ask to see profiles of anyone in a certain age range (but not younger than eighteen) and a certain number of miles from a specific zip code. For example, within 5 miles of my zip code, there were 802 teen women between the ages of eighteen and twenty and 1,031 men. Although many of the pages were innocent enough, some of them were pretty sexually suggestive. MySpace does not allow nudity, but an image can still be sexually explicit without involving nudity. I found sites with names like "D-knockers," "Lips of an angel," and "Alex oso fine." One girl's site slogan said, "My friends say I am crazy and I agree" and posted a picture of her in panties that said across her behind, "you are 83% easy." Another's said, "I love to party, I smoke weed, and I play doctor in my underwear." The young men's sites (all under the legal drinking age of twenty-one) often showed them with beers or liquor bottles in their hands, and many contained alarmingly sexist messages—for example: "Battered women? Sounds delishes." I felt as though I had wandered into some bizarre underground escort service. No one verifies whether these may be younger teens posing as older adolescents.

Some teenagers are clearly misusing these sites. Almost 4 in 10 say that they have given out personal information on these sites, such as their last name or information about their parents or their schools. One-third of teens in one study said they'd pretended to be older than they actually are to get into a Web site. A recent *New York Times* article talked about how some teens are now trying to become famous (or is that infamous?) by posting videos of themselves engaging in outrageous behavior, such as fighting and "fence bashing." YouTube has opened up new possibilities for attention—and for getting into serious trouble. Teenagers have always pulled stupid pranks; but now, they may receive police attention because their deeds are posted online for the entire world to see.

But are these sites dangerous for your child? The answer for the vast majority of users is probably not. Because these sites are relatively new, there has been almost no research on them. For example, the Division of Violence Prevention at the U.S. Centers for Disease Control could not tell me how many youth offline encounters with people they met online were responsible for abductions, rapes, and murders. But they do know that overall cases of missing children and child sexual abuse are down, which means that these sites are not causing an increase in these behaviors. There are more than 100 million users on MySpace alone; if it posed a huge risk to young people's safety, we'd know it by now.

Stories on *Dateline* about online predators and newspaper headlines about older men raping teenage girls they met online are scary. What are these underage girls doing meeting people offline they don't know? Where were their parents? It's simple: meetings with sex offenders are 100 percent preventable if young people do not give out personal identifying information and never go to meet someone offline whom they've met online. One of our local middle schools has posted this adage on their Web site: "Tell your children you love them. If you don't, there is no shortage of pedophiles on the Internet who are eager to."

Fernandes says that parents should be less worried about the forty- or fifty-year-old potential sex offender their teen might meet online than about the twenty- to twenty-four-year-old looking for easy relationships and easy sex with younger lonely partners. The data bear him out: in a national study, one-third of the people sexually soliciting teenagers were between the ages of eighteen and twenty-five. These slightly older young adults seem worldly and often have money to offer a fourteen- or fifteen-year-old. They go on these social networking sites regularly looking for "friends." Your child needs to know that it's not safe to allow people they don't know on their site.

Cell Phones

In our home, we have three cell phones, two landlines, and one fax line. I met a mother of three who has twelve phone lines in her house. With the ubiquity of phones and phone numbers, parents often wonder when to buy their children their own cell phones. And once they've made that decision, they worry about how to monitor their use. After all, when we were teens, we probably had one telephone line. Our parents knew everyone who was calling us, had a chance to interact with our friends, and had the ability to decide if we could take a phone call or not. When children have their own cell phones, that level of monitoring is almost impossible.

If your child doesn't have a cell phone yet, there is a good chance he or she will have one in the near future; according to the Kaiser Family Foundation study, 45 percent of teens have cell phones. But the answer to when your child should have a cell phone is, "It depends." Does your tween have a lot of extracurricular activities after school when you need to be able to reach each other?

There are special cell phones for children that allow calls only to 911 and to and from the numbers that parents preprogram, at preprogrammed times. These phones can be a good idea if your child spends a lot of time alone or if you are frequenting a public place where he or she could get separated from you. Urban middle schoolers who travel alone on buses and subways would surely benefit from having such a phone. And cell phones seem like a downright necessity once your teen begins to drive.

Some cell phones can now be programmed to let you know your child's whereabouts. Placing a locator on your child's cell phone, however, is more about your fears than his or her safety. Several services allow you to link your cell phone to your child's and track the location. It works like the GPS system in some cars, and it enables you to find out within thirty seconds where your child is. Of course, the child's phone has to be on. He or she would receive a text message at the same time, which says, "I m looking 4 u." This system brings up the matter of trust and setting rules, once again. When my son and I talked about these systems, he said, "Why do you need the tracking system? Couldn't you just text-message the kid? I'm supposed to call you if I'm going to be late anyway."

Some of the phones also have a "safety check" feature. For example, you can set the phone to send you a text message at the time your child arrives at a specific location, such as arriving at school or returning home after school. Most phones also have a text-messaging feature. Some teens are more likely to message than to call. If you are not familiar with the text-messaging capabilities of your phones, ask a teenager for help.

Text messaging can be a great parenting aid. A third of teens use IM or text messaging to communicate with their parents. In fact, this feature could be a lifesaver. What if your teen could send you a text message from a party that said, "Mom, there are no parents here. I am going to say I feel sick. Come get me." In one recent case, a girl who was abducted used her cell phone to text-message her parents with her location.

WHAT AFFIRMING PARENTS CAN DO

It's important to have rules to monitor your children's media use. The Kaiser study found that when parents do have rules that they enforce, their children "spend substantially less time using electronic media and more time reading than children whose parents do not take these steps."

Television

1. Set limits.

Young people in homes where parents set limits on television do watch about an hour less of TV a day than children in homes where there are no such limits. They are more likely to read and spend more time on homework as well.

2. Watch with your children.

I don't believe that children under the age of twelve should be watching television on their own. Once you move beyond the PBS years, most television shows contain too much sexual and violent content for your children to watch without mediation.

Watching television with your child provides you with ample teachable moments about sexuality, relationships, community, and the world. You can use programs like *Naked Brothers Band, Gilmore Girls*, and *Zoey 101* to talk with your children (during the breaks, not the shows!) about how people of character would respond in these situations. It may be easier for your tweens or teens to talk about Rory's decisions on *Gilmore Girls* than their own or their friends' decisions. After the age of twelve, you will need to decide about supervising what they watch. My son likes reality television shows, and they offer a lot of opportunities to talk about how people make both good and bad decisions.

I do think that limits such as "no television before chores and homework" make sense, and I think that parents have the right to make overly sexualized or overly violent programs off-limits, at least until high school. Our family guideline is that you can watch any TV or movie that you want, but if it is rated TV-14 or R, you have to watch with a parent and you have to be willing to have "teachable moment time" afterward. That's not so easy when it comes to use of the personal computer.

Computers and the Internet

Despite growing concerns about Internet use, most parents set very few limits. In the Kaiser Family Foundation 2003 study, only 1 in 4 parents had rules for what their kids could do on the computer, including limits on how much time could be spent and what content could be accessed. Three-quarters of young people in seventh through twelfth grades say that their home computer does not have a filter or parental controls.

1. Put the computer in a public place.

This is Rule Number One for Affirming Parents. The most important way we can supervise our children's and teens' Internet use is to put the computer they use in a space where we can see it. Although three-quarters of teens say that the computer with Internet access is in a family area, more than one-quarter say that they have Internet access in their bedroom. In general, this is not a good idea. If you want to be able to monitor your child's use of the Internet, have the computer in the family room, den, living room, or kitchen.

I highly recommend setting your e-mail account to include a spam filter, but even so, I probably receive several e-mails a day for sexual medications and dating services even at my church e-mail account. Your children and teens are receiving these, too, and they need to know that they should always delete any messages from someone they do not know without opening them.

Filters are a good idea if your child is twelve or younger, but for older children, they just limit their access to information they may need to access. For example, most of the filters will block the American Cancer Society because it teaches breast and testicular self-exam. They definitely block out all the good sex education sites for teenagers. Most technologically savvy teenagers know how to get around them anyway.

Rather than filters for children over twelve, give your children and younger teens the message that they should let you know if they come across anything online that disturbs them. Searching sometimes does take you to unexpected sexualized sites. When he was in seventh grade, Greg came into my office after school looking ashen one day after searching for a picture for the cover of his news report on Hurricane Katrina. He had Google-imaged the word *Katrina* expecting to find scenes of hurricane devastation. Instead, he came upon a page full of images of half-dressed women in sultry poses. Who knew that would happen? Fortunately Greg was comfortable enough to talk to me about the sexually explicit sites that had popped up in his search. He also knew our agreement that I periodically check his "history file," and he did not want me to think that he had visited these sites voluntarily.

2. Know the technology yourself, and know what your child is doing.

If you are not at ease on the Internet, it's time to take a course or have your child teach you. You cannot monitor what you do not understand. If you are at ease on the Internet but unfamiliar with social networking sites, start by asking your tween or teen if they have a Web page. We were at the home of friends last summer when I asked their fifteen-year-old daughter if she had a page on MySpace. She paled and stuttered that she did. It was obvious her parents didn't know about it, or even know what the site was. I think the girl has been mad at me ever since. My friend was not alone, though; 38 percent of parents have never seen their teenagers' online profile.

3. If your child tells you that he or she has a Web page, ask to see it—tomorrow.

Give your child time to clean up the site. When I shared this suggestion with Mr. Fernandes, he cautioned me that your child may have multiple pages. He said, "In an hour, your child can create a 'princess page' with nothing but bland content. That does not mean she won't have another page." In fact, he asserts, "if a child wants to keep something from a parent on MySpace, the parent will never know." Try asking directly how many online accounts they have or whether there is a second page.

Request that your teenager lock the account, which prohibits people from visiting a page without the owner's permission. MySpace allows users to designate their profiles as private and allow e-mail only from a named list of friends.

4. Get your own account on MySpace, and ask your child to allow you to become a friend on his or her account.

But ask your child for help in designing your page so that it is not embarrassing to link to you. This can backfire, though. Some parents put up pages and get bombarded by their children's friends, sending silly messages or "Can I be your friend?" messages. It's called "friend bombing."

5. Agree on rules for social networking site use.

MySpace offers its own rules for its younger users, which include:

• Do not forget that this is a public space. Do not post anything you do not want the world to know.

• Do not make it easy for a stranger to find you.

• People are not always who they say they are. Be careful about adding strangers to your "friends" lists.

• Report harassment, hate speech, and inappropriate content.

• Do not mislead people into thinking you are older or younger.

A number of Web sites, which are listed in the Appendix, suggest limits for safe Internet use, including:

• Be sure your children agree never to meet someone offline whom they have met online, unless you're with them. This is probably the most important guideline of all. If your child is over sixteen and does not agree to have you come, at least have him or her agree to meet people in a very public place and to bring some friends along. Make sure they agree to tell you before they do this and to send you a text message that they are all right. But I'd discourage any such meetings until they are at least out of high school.

- Encourage your children to come to you with any problems they encounter online.
- Limit the amount of time your children can be on social networking sites, say, to thirty minutes or an hour a day. Just like Internet surfing or blog reading, they can become a black hole. A good limit might be no Internet until homework is done—although many teens use the Internet for homework, IM'ing the whole time they're online. No IMs while doing homework might be another rule in your home.
- Visit your child's Web page once a week or so, and leave a friend's message.
- Be sure that no identifying details are included: no school names, sports teams' names, the town they live in, or where they hang out.
- Look at the photos to see if they inadvertently give clues to personal information. A picture of your teen in front of a school building is not a good idea.
- Talk to them about their screen names. They should not be too sexualized (nastygrl is one recent example I found of a fourteen-year-old) or give away too much information (stevewest-on15 could be easy to track).
- Make sure your children are being honest about their age. Sites have age rules for good reasons. If your child is too young for a particular site, talk to him or her about alternatives.
- Ask your children or teens to think about the messages they are posting and what message they might be giving someone who isn't their friend. "I am lonely," "I hate my life," and "I love playing doctor" are the types of messages that offenders are looking for in deciding whom to groom for a relationship.
- Have them use the protection features on their account; for example, they want to be able to moderate comments from friends before they're posted. This cuts down on public bullying, but also keeps your child from being linked to sites they don't want to be linked to.
- Remind your children not to post photos they wouldn't want you or their grandmother to see. Embarrassing photos can be copied onto other people's sites and may have a much longer

life on the Internet than young people think. Ask them to consider if they would want a college admissions officer or potential employer to see the picture.

6. Set and maintain consequences when limits are broken.

The natural consequences for violating the agreed-upon limits seem pretty obvious to me: take away access to the computer for a specified amount of time, depending on the severity of the infraction. For example, it is much more serious to find out that your teen has gone to meet someone without your permission than that he or she didn't not lock the account. If I found out that Greg had a Web page that he was hiding from us, I would see that as a pretty serious violation of our trust and would limit his online access at home to supervised homework time. If you find that your children are abusing their IM account, you could make them shut it down for three or four weeks. Check to be sure that it's been done. Discuss potential consequences with your child or teen in advance for violating your home's agreement about Internet use.

But recognize that you can only monitor your child's Internet use at home. Your tween and teen has access to the Internet at school, at the public library, at most community centers these days, and at their friends' homes. There is almost no way to completely monitor their use. That is where a trusting relationship comes in. They may also have access to the Internet on their handhelds and their cell phones, although in a time of consequences, you may also be able to block their access on their portable equipment.

Cell Phones

1. Make sure your child knows the basic rules.

As with every other area I've discussed, you will want to establish some rules and guidelines with your child or teen for cell phone use. Make sure they know to:

- Give their number out only to people they know and trust.
- Not reply to text messages from people they don't know.
- Use the blocking mechanism for people they don't want to call.

2. Set limits for use.

Make clear the times when there is to be absolutely no cell phone use, including at school, while doing homework, or while the family is eating dinner. Some families agree that everyone in the family, including the adults, will turn off their phones or charge them during the dinner hour. Some parents suggest that teens turn off their phones all evening and receive calls only through the family's landline. While you're at it, ban iPods at dinner as well. Family dinners should serve as opportunities for discussion.

3. Agree on consequences.

Again, the potential consequences for violating your agreed-upon limits are pretty obvious: take away the cell phone for a specific period of time, depending on the severity of the violation. You can also check the histories on the bills to see how your child is using the phone, but I would recommend doing this only if you have a clear concern. That brings us to the question of how closely to supervise and monitor your child's cell phone and computer use.

To Snoop or Not to Snoop in the Wireless Age

Parents have always had to resist the temptation to read their children's and teens' mail, journals, or notes left in jeans tossed into the wash. But cell phone histories, e-mails, and IMs left up on the screen make it easier not just to keep tabs on your children but to invade their privacy as well.

I recently saw a full-page ad by the organization Parents: The Anti-Drug with a large banner headline that read: "It is a fine line between respecting your teen's privacy and doing your job as a parent." It is a topic that comes up during the question-and-answer section of most of my parenting talks, as well. Someone inevitably asks, "Should I be spying on my teenager online?"

My quick answer is *no*. Affirming Parents want to develop trusting relationships with our children. Just as we should not be reading their journals and letters or combing through their drawers, we should not be reading their private online correspondence, either. Would you open a letter that came to your teenage child without their knowing about it? Why should mail sent electronically be any different? Do you listen in on your child's or teen's phone calls without their knowing? Then why would you read their IM logs? (As I mentioned in the drugs chapter, all bets are off if you suspect your child of being involved with illegal or physically harmful behavior. In those cases, tell your child you plan to check his or her computer use.)

There are actually computer programs you can use to check in on your teens' computer use. Several programs are legal for parents to put on their teens' computers (but not their spouse's or employees') that will capture every keystroke. They give you full access to your children's e-mails, IMs, and every Web site visited. One technology records chats, keystrokes typed, and the names of Web sites visited, and will e-mail you as often as every thirty minutes with a report of where your teen or child has visited online. Your child or teen does not even have to know the program has been installed.

These programs make me uncomfortable. Do you want to spy on your children without their permission or monitor them every thirty minutes during your workday? There is a big difference in my mind between snooping or spying on your child and using appropriate parental monitoring and supervision. Setting clear limits and outlining the consequences are the Affirming Parent's approach. (Go back and look at pages 159 to 163 to see possible guidelines for you and your child to discuss about Internet use.)

Wiredsafety.org, a Web-based organization on Internet safety, has an interesting take on these products. They say, "Install it and forget it. If and when something horrible happens or your child is being targeted by a cyber bully, it will already have collected the evidence you need in a form law enforcement can use. It is the security camera in the corner of the local bank. And priceless when you need to trace someone who hurt you or your children online." I guess they have a point, but I'm still not going to buy one. Setting guidelines, limits, and consequences makes more sense to me, as well as trusting that my son will come to me if he is disturbed by something that happens online—just as I trust he will come to me if something disturbing happens to him offline. Remember, we are trying to reinforce our growing children's independent decision-making capabilities.

It is also important to recognize that even if you have these programs on your home computer, they can't tell you what your child or teen is doing on the Internet at school, the library, on their cell phones, or anywhere else. No amount of "snoopware" is going to tell you everything.

I have received many calls from parents telling me that they have "discovered" sexually explicit IM conversations left on their preteen's or teen's computers and wonder what to do. They are usually shocked by the sexually sophisticated language and abashedly admit that they turned on their teens' private computer to see what they were doing. The easiest way to avoid this problem is to follow Rule Number One discussed earlier: keep family computers in public places.

But if you do come across something like this, it's really no different from reading your child's notes or journal. If you find something that really disturbs you, either accidentally or on purpose, you are going to have to address it with your child, even if it means apologizing for the privacy violation at the same time. Begin by telling your child that the IM was left up and that you read it. You can say something like, "I'm sorry I read your IMs, but I'm even more concerned about the language you were using and the acts that you were discussing. I'd like to talk more about this." Be sure to share your values and your household rules about computer use. Try to remember that teens who use sexually sophisticated language in IMs or on a social networking site may not be engaging in such behavior offline. It may be a type of rehearsal play.

The best advice I can offer is to think before you snoop. You may not like what you find, and you may end up undermining your child's trust. The point is that we need to be raising children and teens whom we trust and who can trust us. The new technology does not have to change that. We also want to raise children who make ethical decisions and contribute positively to the world, which the final chapter will address.

CHAPTER 10

Raising a Mensch: The Importance of Ethics and Spirituality in Your Child's World

MENSCH IS A Yiddish word that literally means "a human being," but it implies a person with a strong moral character. Leo Rosten, in *The Joys of Yiddish*, said a mensch is "someone to admire and emulate, someone of noble character. The key to being a real mensch is nothing less than character, rectitude, dignity, a sense of what is right, responsible, decorous."

We want our children to be healthy, happy, successful, and safe, but the core of what many of us want most is for our children to be "nice." We want them to kind, decent human beings who are compassionate and empathic. We want them to make ethical decisions, and many of us want them to develop their spirituality and a commitment to our particular faith.

We want our children to thrive. The Search Institute uses the term *thriving* to refer to a teen who "not only grows and flourishes as an individual, but also contributes to family, community, and society." They write that "thriving youth show evidence not only of the absence of negative behaviors but also of indicators of positive development, such as school engagement, commitment to helping others, positive adult relationships, self-esteem, overcoming adversity, and valuing diversity." They may not use this word, but I think they are talking about mensches.

We want our children to be spiritual and moral, but many of today's baby-boom and early Gen X parents do not want to force our children into our own religious beliefs. Often that's because we have negative memories of being forced to sit through stifling church or synagogue experiences when *we* were children. Indeed, the percentage of young people being raised without a religious identity has nearly tripled since the early 1990s, although it is still just 14 percent. (Again, reverse the statistic to see that 86 percent of children are being raised to identify with a religious tradition.)

The vast majority of married couples and parents today report a religious affiliation, just as our parents did, and 9 in 10 desire religious training for their children. Many parents return to an organized religious community after a long absence because of a desire to offer their children a structure for moral values and meaning. It was only after we had our first child that my husband and I began to search for a religious community that would respect our different past faith traditions. In my denomination, we even have a joke about this: "What is a Unitarian Universalist? An atheist with children."

Many of today's parents self-identify as "spiritual, not religious," reflecting some people's desire to seek meaning without what they see as the confines of organized religion. Harvard psychologist Dr. Robert Coles, who has spent his life researching and writing about moral development, said in his book *The Ongoing Journey: Awakening Spiritual Life in At-Risk Youth* that spirituality is "to wonder about life and try to figure it out." In his seminal book *The Spiritual Life of Children*, he wrote that all children hunger for the answers to spiritual questions: "Where do we come from? Why are we here? What is the meaning of life?"

Others agree that the search for the answers to these questions is universal, even to the point of being "hardwired" into us. The Institute for American Values, in a 2002 publication called "Hardwired to Connect: The Scientific Case for Authoritative Communities," says: "We are hardwired for other people and for moral meaning and openness to the transcendent. Meeting those basic needs for connection is essential to health and to human flourishing."

Indeed, many observers and educators believe that children, with or without religious instruction, seem to have an innate curiosity about spiritual issues. Anyone who has spent time with a two- or three-year-old knows that they have a sense of wonder, an appreciation for nature, a delightful spontaneity, and a creative imagination. They want to know why the sky is blue, where the flowers come from, why that man is in a wheelchair, where they were before they were born, and why pets and people have to die. They can seem endlessly curious about the world around them.

As they get older, especially in today's world, they are faced with ever more complex faith questions. Any of us who has discussed 9/11, the Indonesian tsunami, Hurricane Katrina, or a relative with cancer with our elementary school and older children knows that our children are not immune from trying to make sense of suffering. They have the same questions we do: Why do bad things happen to good people? Why is life unfair? Why is there hate? Why do some good people have to die young?

We should not avoid discussing difficult issues or disasters, natural and otherwise, with our children, because they need our help to understand them. Those of us who had young children on September 11, 2001, wanted to protect them from the horror but soon realized it was impossible to shield them from the news, the conversations, other children, and the grief of the adults around them. (We could, however, keep them from the ubiquitous TV images of the planes being flown into the Twin Towers.) These horrifying events require us to use them as teachable moments and to do our best to reassure our children that they are safe.

Dr. James Fowler, a professor at the Candler School of Theology, pioneered what he labeled "faith development theory" to explain how faith develops in a person over a lifetime. He believes that faith is a universal need that all of us have, inside and outside of religion. He wrote that faith underlies "the formation of the belief, values, and meanings that give coherence and direction to person's lives...and enable them to face and deal with the challenges of human life and death, relying on that which has the quality of ultimacy in their lives."

Using that definition, we can understand why it is important for parents to nurture their children's faith. We want our children to have a clear sense of their own values and beliefs, and many of us hope to

develop those within the faith structures of our family. Fowler identi-
fies the stage of faith in middle childhood as "mythic literal faith."
Understanding that children are concrete thinkers, this is the age for
parents and faith leaders to use stories, narratives, and myths to share
their religious beliefs. The "middle child" is concerned, in Fowler's
words, with "simple fairness and moral reciprocity."

Moral reciprocity is actually the ethical cornerstone of many of
the world's religions; you may know it as the Golden Rule. The Dalai
Lama has written, "Every religion emphasizes human improvement,
love, respect for others, sharing other people's suffering." Late elementary school is the ideal time to instill the Golden Rule expressed
in so many of the world's religions: "Do unto others as you would
have them do onto you," which was expressed by Plato in the fourth
century as, "May I do unto others as I would that they should do
unto me." Judaism and Christianity teach, "Love thy neighbor as
thyself"; Buddhism teaches, "Hurt not others in ways that you would
yourself find hurtful"; and Islam that "None of you truly believes
until he wishes for his brother what he wishes for himself." It is a
good place to start with your eight- to twelve-year-old.

In a beautiful passage in his 1979 book, titled *Faith and Belief*,
Wilfred Cantwell Smith, a well-known world religions scholar,
wrote:

> *Faith, then, is a quality of human living. At its best, it has
> taken the form of serenity and courage and loyalty and serv-
> ice; a quiet confidence and joy which enable one to feel at
> home in the universe, and to find meaning in the world and
> in one's own life, a meaning that is profound and ultimate,
> and is stable no matter what may happen to oneself at the
> level of immediate event. Men and women of this kind of
> faith face catastrophe and confusion, affluence and sorrow,
> unperturbed; face opportunity with conviction and drive; and
> face others with cheerful charity.*

Read it again slowly. This is a very tall order, and one that I'm
not sure many people, including religious leaders, attain, especially that part about the ability to face catastrophe unperturbed. But
it is a lovely goal if one thinks about equipping one's child with

that kind of peace, confidence, joy, and stability in approaching life.

That is why thinking about how to raise spiritually healthy children should be a goal for *all* Affirming Parents, not just those who practice a religion themselves. Faith is not the same thing as subscribing to a specific set of beliefs or religious teachings or participating in a faith-based community. One can nurture a child's faith and spirit without belonging to a faith tradition, although for many of us, faith traditions provide a context. You do not have to be religious, spiritual, or belong to a faith community to affirm that as a parent, you have the responsibility to guide your children in their search for meaning, in an understanding of how to make ethical decisions, and in answering the big questions they have about life.

Is it tougher for today's parents to do this than in previous generations? I don't think so. Yes, the specter of terrorism looms in our background, but the cold war and the threat of nuclear annihilation did so in earlier years. Yes, the world seems more commercialized and the media more inevitable as an educator of children, but that makes it more, not less, important to consider our roles in helping nurture spiritually healthy children.

THE AFFIRMING PARENT'S ROLE IN SPIRITUAL AND ETHICAL DEVELOPMENT

As in almost every area I have discussed in this book, parental modeling of healthy, ethical behaviors makes a difference. Dr. Robert Coles, in *The Moral Intelligence of Children*, wrote that what is most important to children is observing the important adults in their lives: "The witness of our lives, our ways of being with others and speaking to them and getting on with them—all that taken in slowly, cumulatively, by our own sons and daughters...in the long run of a child's life, the unself-conscious moments that are what we think of simply as the unfolding events of the day and the week turn out to be the powerful and persuasive times, morally."

How we respond to the "big questions" that children ask is part of their faith development. In my work with parents on sexuality issues, I often reassure them that the sex questions that have scientific answers (such as "Where do I come from?" or "But how did the baby get in there?") are much easier to answer than the theological questions ("Why was I born?"; "Where do people go after they die?"; "Why do bad things happen?"). When Greg was four, I found it much easier to respond to "How come girls do not have penises?" than to his question as we drove by the cemetery, "How come people have to die?"

Authoritarian Parents often supply children with the answers, cutting off discussion or telling them what to believe. Affirming Parents try to encourage their child's sense of faith and wonder and understand that these types of questions are an opportunity for dialogue and discussions, not lectures. Parents can start by asking, "Well, what do you think?" rather than rushing in with answers. Moral reasoning is enhanced when parents ask their children questions to discuss their approach to a situation or question. Affirming Parents acknowledge the mysteries of life ("No one knows for sure") while sharing parts of the answers they have found helpful ("It comforts me to believe in heaven"), rather than insisting on shared beliefs. A Jewish preschool has this slogan, which appeals to me: "A child is not a cup to be filled, but a light to be kindled."

I have always been indebted to Anita Hall, who was the director of religious education at our church when Alyssa was in preschool. One of the children asked her one day, "Who is God?" You may have other ways of explaining this to your children at different ages, but what Anita shared with Alyssa's class that day has always stayed with me as the right answer for our family. She said that "God is the happiness that is inside our hearts." It still seems to me like perfect preschool theology, and it speaks to many adults as well.

My denomination, the Unitarian Universalist Association, is based on seven principles that we then translate into concrete language for our children. I offer the child's version here, not for you necessarily to adopt in your family but for you to think about ethical principles you'd want to share with your children. They are:

- Each and every person is important.
- All people should be treated fairly and kindly.
- We should encourage one another and learn together.

- Each person must be free to search for what is true and right in life.
- All persons should have a say about the things that concern them.
- We should work together for a peaceful, fair, and free world.
- We should care for our planet earth, the home we share with all living things.

You might want to think through what core values you want to share with your children and teenagers. And then think about whether your family life reflects those values. As Kahlil Gibran wrote almost one hundred years ago, "Your daily life is your temple and your religion."

The point here is not to offer you my answers but to encourage you to think about how you want to handle these types of discussions with your own children. Parents often shy away from these types of discussions because they mistakenly believe that their children are too young to understand them. It is important to honor your children's questions and to take them seriously. That means you first need to think about what it is *you* believe about these important issues. It is helpful to share your doubts and questions and offer your children the answers as you know and understand them. But Affirming Parents know it is best to encourage conversation and dialogue with their children.

These types of conversations are not just about the big questions of life and faith but also about moral decision making, respect, empathy and justice. Just as with sex and drugs, there are "teachable moments" that arise every day to discuss moral issues with your children about your family's ethics and values. The news, television, movies, and their own experiences at school provide you with seemingly endless moments to address your family's values about such issues as diversity, fairness, tolerance, and equality. The front page of your local newspaper will give you plenty of ideas.

Barbara Levi-Berliner, my colleague and a social worker, tells all her parenting groups, "Children are perceivers, not interpreters." In other words, they pick up almost everything going on in their environment but often do not understand what they perceive. This may involve something in the larger world, but it also may be actions going on in your own household. She told me the story of a five-year-old girl who had gone from being delightful to being a holy terror at home. When she asked the girl's mother if anything had changed at home, the mother responded, "No, nothing has changed. Oh, well I am five months' pregnant—but there's no way she knows that yet." Barbara suggested to this mom that she and her husband talk to the little girl about becoming a big sister; once they shared the news and started including their daughter in preparations for the new baby, the difficult behavior stopped. Her daughter knew *something* important was going on in the family, and she needed to be let in on it.

But in their larger world, children are often exposed to issues long before we are ready for them to be. Nonetheless, once they go to preschool or kindergarten or turn on the television instead of a parent-approved video, it's difficult if not impossible to protect them from the world. Leaving church one day, I overheard a discussion in which a mother asked her eight-year-old son what they had talked about in Sunday school. Her son said, "Terrorists." The mother, looking worried, asked, "Honey, what is a terrorist?" He replied, "Someone who likes visiting other countries." She answered, with great relief in her voice, "No, honey, that is a *tourist*." But he had indeed heard the word *terrorist* somewhere, maybe even at home.

Parents at my sexuality talks often ask me how they can protect their child's innocence. "Surely," they say to me, "you agree that children receive sexualized messages too early today." Yes, children are bombarded by sexually exploitative messages perhaps more than ever before. But it is a myth to think that you can protect your child completely. You can turn off the television, but there's not much you can do about the advertisements in the newspapers or the billboards that they also may see. If you take your child to the grocery store, in the checkout line he or she will see the covers of the women's magazines. Not only do these magazines often show women in various states of undress, but they often feature cover story headlines such as "The Top Ten Sex Secrets Men Wish You Knew" or "Helping Your Husband Last Longer." And then there are the tabloids a little closer to the cashier. My favorite headline ever in one of those blared to my then seven-year-old, "Lesbian Aliens Impregnate Oprah." Unless you can keep your children locked inside your carefully protected home, they are likely to be exposed to such messages over and over.

Your job as a parent is to help mediate these messages and communicate your family values. Rather than ignoring them, use them as teachable moments to give your child a little bit of information or to share your values. "Honey, it makes me uncomfortable to see grown women dressed in tiny outfits. Why do you think she is dressed this way?" "Sweetie, wasn't that headline silly?"

These discussions about moral quandaries and issues are also a way to help your children develop the ability to make ethical decisions for themselves, a skill they will need to deal with all the issues I have discussed in this book. Affirming Parents know that a mixture of limits and freedom to make age-appropriate choices is the foundation for a lifetime of moral decision making.

So, how do we raise mensches? Through modeling ethical behaviors ourselves, talking with our children about justice issues, teaching them to treat all people with dignity and respect (and treating our children and others that way), and encouraging their spiritual, moral, and faith development.

WHAT AFFIRMING PARENTS CAN DO

1. Listen to your children.

Listening to your children and showing them empathy helps them develop their own sense of compassion. All people want empathy, even children. They want to know that they have been heard. Dr. Marshall B. Rosenberg, the founder of the Center for Nonviolent Communication, writes that children need an "empathic kind of connection...a respectful understanding where the child feels that we are there and hear what he or she is feeling and needing." This can be done through nonverbal communication in your facial expression or by giving your child a hug or touch, but it can also be done by verbally letting your child know that he or she has been heard.

In an example in his book *Raising Children Compassionately*, Dr. Rosenberg asks people to think about how to respond to a child who says, for example, "Nobody likes me." Some parents jump in too fast with reassurance ("Well, that is not true; you've had friends in the past. I am sure you will get more friends") or advice ("Maybe if you'd talk differently to your friends, your friends would like you more"). Instead, he recommends that parents say something empathic, such as, "So it sounds like you're feeling sad, because you are not having very much fun with your friends." Modeling compassion and empathy in the adult relationships in your home teaches your children as well.

2. Learn from your children.

Of course, our children can be our spiritual teachers as well. One of the central teachings I have learned from my children is the importance of living in the moment. I remember one beautiful spring day when my daughter was about four and I wanted us to go for a "signs of spring" walk. I drove to a park near our house. We stepped out of the car, and she immediately saw a rock that she liked. We stopped. We went another two feet. There was a stick to pick up. We took another step or two, and there was a dandelion to be looked at, smelled, its petals to be pulled out. I found myself getting impatient; I wanted to take her to the bridge deeper into the park, I wanted to get some exercise, and we were supposed to be on a walk, not a step-and-stop! Two more steps and she saw a ladybug on a stick, moving slowly, glinting in the sun. We watched it slowly inch from one end to the other. Another step, dirt to run through her fingers. A half hour later, we still had not made it to the official beginning of the path. And then, of course, I got it: *this* was our "signs of spring" walk.

3. Establish family rituals.

Some of my friends say that they went to bed every night by the prayer "Now I Lay Me Down to Sleep" and to this day repeat it before going to bed. Establishing rituals helps to nurture your children's sense of spirituality. These can include daily rituals, such as moments of gratitude before meals or blessings at bedtime. How your family celebrates religious holidays is part of ritual observance and provides children with a sense of faith security: rituals can range from attending your faith community's holiday service to how you celebrate birthdays and report cards. We have been cutting down our holiday tree with the same family friends for the past eighteen years; it is as much a part of the winter holiday season as going to church on Christmas Eve. We also celebrate Jewish holidays to honor my family's heritage. First night Seder is always at Grandpa's; my not-so-great potato latkes at Hannukah are a must. What family traditions do you celebrate in your home?

We can also develop rituals for secular events. Some parents come up with a special gift or dinner to give their daughter to mark her first menstrual period. I have held "last carry" ceremonies with both of our children. I realized that several important moments at the end of their babyhood had happened without being marked (the last time they breastfed; the day they gave up diapers), so I wanted to mark this transition from toddlerhood to childhood. Around age five or six, as each became too heavy for me to lift and carry, I picked them up for the last time, carried them around their rooms, and placed them down with a blessing for the "last carry."

My dear friend Kate Hanley came up with another special ritual that we followed for our own children. Her children's friends had begun preparing for their bar and bat mitzvahs in the fourth grade, and their parents had begun planning the celebrations. Kate realized that her Christian children would not have such events to celebrate their move to maturity, so she created the "first decade party" for their tenth birthday. She and her children identified the teachers, babysitters, neighbors, and friends who had been important parts of her child's life. Each was asked to bring a scrapbook page with memories of her child's first decade. At the party, people were asked to share their memories of the child's first decade. Pictures were taken and placed in the scrapbook.

Many such moments can be celebrated by rituals with your children. Do you do something special on the first day of school each year? My sister has taken a picture of each of her children on the front porch every year of their school lives. They made a great collage. What happens in your family when your child loses a tooth?

Is there something special you do every year on the last day of school? Think about other events that you can celebrate with a family ritual. Use your imagination to create lasting memories with your child.

Rituals can be either secular or religious. Instead of prayers before meals, each family member can share one good thing from their day. Bedtime rituals can include parents offering a special way of saying good night and an affirmation of love that children can learn to count on, and that can be sent in messages or on the telephone as they begin to spend time away from home.

I devised this nightly blessing when my daughter was only a few weeks old: "May the angels watch over you tonight. May God bless you. I love you."

I have said it every night since, first to Alyssa and then to Greg. I have sent it in e-mail messages, whispered it on the phone when they have been at sleepovers and camp, and even on cell phone answering services during Alyssa's semesters abroad. I have said it to them before medical procedures, first days of school, and a driving test. I have even sent it in a text message. These simple words that they have heard all their lives comfort them; they comfort me in the offering, and connect our love to something bigger than we are. You may want to write such a blessing for your family. You do not need to believe in God or angels or even prayer; you can address the universe or the sacred within all of us, or just concentrate on your shared love. You can adapt or use your own tradition's prayers: Jewish and Christian parents, for example, could use the benediction, "May God bless you and protect you. May God shine upon you with graciousness. May God look upon you with favor and grant you peace." You could develop this special saying together as a family project.

Prayers with your children will vary by tradition but can nurture your child's sense of spirituality if they are consistent with your tradition. A thirteenth-century German theologian named Meister Eckardt wrote that the only prayer we ever need is "thank you." More recently Christian writer Anne Lamott said that the only prayers we ever need are "thank you, thank you, thank you" and "help me, help me, help me." I have heard people quote Rabbi Marc Gelman and

Monsignor Thomas Harman as saying that the only prayers children need are "thanks, gimme, wow, and oops."

4. Celebrate traditions in community.

Celebrating traditions in community also provides a spiritual home for your children. It will not surprise you to know that as a minister, I believe in the power of an organized faith community to offer meaning and support in your and your children's lives. I consider myself, like the majority of Americans, both religious and spiritual. Although we can pray alone, it is in community that we find support and opportunities for action. Hillary Rodham Clinton made popular the African expression "It takes a village to raise a child." Often the faith community can be such a village for parents.

5. Consider the role of a faith community.

Ralph and I began to search for a faith community when our daughter was about three. I come from a fairly secular Jewish family; his family is Roman Catholic. We had developed our traditions around meals; Ralph used to joke that "we ate our religion." In other words, we had Rosh Hashanah dinner with chicken soup and matzo balls, the seven-fish Italian Christmas Eve dinner, latkes at Hannukah, ham at Easter, and so on. But we also recognized that we wanted our children to know about both of their religious heritages and to feel that they belonged to a religious tradition. Interfaith couples of any mix often need to consciously decide which faith community might best fit with their family; others go back and forth between two.

Finding a faith community that meets your family's spiritual and religious needs is important. For some of us that means finding the church or synagogue that is affiliated with the denomination of our own childhood. For others it means seeking a new faith. Meeting with the person in charge of religious education can be an important first step. How are children valued in the life of the faith community? How are they included or not included in worship? What is covered in Sunday school? What are the requirements for attendance? How are the teachers trained, and how does the faith community screen its leaders and keep children safe from sexual abuse? How is diversity valued, and how are children involved in the intergenerational aspects of the community? What are the community's beliefs and values about current social issues? Are there opportunities for community service or mission trips?

Modeling the role of faith in our homes and in our lives is important. For those of us who belong to faith communities, that means attending family church, mosque, or synagogue regularly, saying prayers before meals and bedtime, participating in service projects as a family, and discussing our faith. These simple behaviors set a foundation for the role of religion in family life and give our children a solid religious home. Although they may leave the faith community in middle or late adolescence, many will return to it (or choose a different one) when they have their own families. There is some research that suggests that the closer children or teens feel to their parents, the more likely it is that they will accept their family's religion as they grow up. Another reason for family connectiveness.

The majority of tweens and teens in America *are* involved in faith communities, and such involvement actually protects them against some of the behaviors I have discussed in this book. The National Study of Youth and Religion found that more than 8 in 10 teens (82 percent) said that faith was very or somewhat important in shaping their daily lives, and 8 in 10 said that it was very or somewhat important in shaping their major life decisions. Almost 7 in 10 teenagers view themselves as religious (69 percent), and depending on the study, between one-third and one-half report that they attend weekly worship. Almost 4 in 10 (38 percent) are members of a religious youth group.

There is, of course, a difference between young people reporting that they feel religious and those who actually attend a faith community. Youth group leaders routinely bemoan how difficult it is to keep young people engaged in the youth group through their high school years, and many parents worry that their children are giving up on their faith. What is more likely is that they are becoming increasingly involved in other outside activities, and time spent with peers seems more important to them than time spent in worship.

Those young people who do stick with their youth groups are less likely to get involved in risk-taking behaviors. They have lower rates of alcohol and drug use and lower rates of sexual intercourse. Religious teens have half the rate of sexual intercourse than young people in the U.S. Centers for Disease Control study of all teenagers in the United States. The National Study of Youth and Religion has shown that teens who are active in faith communities tend to be physically healthier: they are more likely than nonreligious teens to exercise, to eat well, to use seat belts, and even to floss! But just as important, they also exhibit higher altruism and moral values, and are more likely to volunteer, to be active in afterschool activities, and to have higher grade point averages. Religious high school students are actually three times more likely than other teens to have performed community service.

Of course, there is the chicken-and-egg problem in understanding all these statistics: Does involvement in a religious institution cause these more positive outcomes, or are young people who exhibit them more likely to be involved in faith-based communities? What we do know is that young people's involvement in community service is good for our children and up significantly from a generation ago.

An Ethic of Action: Involve Your Children in Community Service

The Hebrew expression *tikkun olam* means "repair of the world"; in the Book of James in the New Testament, it says, "faith without works is dead." Providing your children with opportunities to be of service is one way to develop a sense of compassion and good character. Two other Hebrew words sum up the sense of responsibility that we can nurture in our children and youth. A *mitzvah* translates as a "good deed." And *gemilut hasadim* means acts of loving kindness. Children can be taught that spirituality, ethical treatment, and social action are intimately connected, whether or not your family practices a particular religion.

Such educational giants of the twentieth century as John Dewey and Jean Piaget wrote that children learn by doing. Involving your children in service to others is an important part of raising them to be caring. Even the youngest children can accompany you to a soup kitchen or on a visit to an elderly neighbor or family member. Signing your family up to feed people at a homeless shelter or helping with a Habitat for Humanity build provides opportunities for family connection and service. Barbara Levi-Berliner's family has spent every Thanksgiving since her children were tiny serving meals at a soup kitchen. Her family eats their Thanksgiving dinner the next day. Alyssa still remembers the years we spent wrapping holiday presents for people with AIDS. Investigate the opportunities for community service in your area.

If you are involved in social action, share it with your children. Alyssa came to her first women's rights rally with me at the age of three; I think Greg was nine. The list of possible volunteer opportunities for upper elementary school children and teenagers is nearly endless: they can tutor younger children, offer free babysitting services, collect food, run recycling drives, assist in food pantries and soup kitchens, paint murals in vacant lots, plant trees and community gardens, and organize neighborhood cleanup projects. They can volunteer at shelters, nursing homes, and hospitals. They can work on fundraisers or even organize them: hold bake sales, car washes, auctions; collect pennies, books, and games; and put on talent shows. Religious institutions may provide volunteer activities for youth, but so can 4-H, Boy and Girl Scouts, and boys' and girls' clubs.

Young people today are actually involved in community service and volunteer projects at higher rates than ever before. The Higher Education Research Institute conducts an annual survey of college freshmen about their attitudes and behaviors. In 2006, more than 8 in 10 college freshmen reported having volunteered at least occasionally, compared with about two-thirds in 1989. Half have participated in a demonstration about a cause, compared with only 1 in 7 in 1966. Applications to the Peace Corps, Vista, and Teach for America are all up significantly. As with almost all the areas I have discussed in this book, the "mensch index" is moving in the right direction. We can congratulate ourselves as parents because we have done a lot of things right.

AFTERWORD

Our Children Are Our Greatest Blessing

ALTHOUGH IT CAN be difficult at times, rather than worrying about today's young people or bemoaning the fast-paced changes in their and our lives, we should be highlighting all the ways that children and teens make better decisions than their parents did when we were young. We should be excited that we have been given the gift of being a parent at the beginning of the twenty-first century.

On the whole, our children are healthier than any previous generation of young people. They are smart, committed, and engaged in their families and their communities. They like their parents and want us to share their lives. They are avoiding dangerous behaviors more than children have for the past fifty years. They are blessed by a world of information at their fingertips and technology that was undreamed of when we were children.

We are lucky to be their parents. Even on those days when we are most stressed out—and I have plenty of those myself—we should try to remember that we are blessed by our children. Although there are no guarantees, Affirming Parents know there is much we can do to raise happy, healthy, and competent children and adolescents who will have productive and satisfying adult lives.

I invite you to share my optimism for today's children and youth. It is in our hands as parents to create the next generation who will carry on the world.

Abraham Lincoln said it well (although I wish he had explicitly included our daughters):

> *A child is a person who is going to carry on what you have started. He is going to sit where you are sitting, and when you are gone, attend to those things which you think are important. You may adopt all the policies you please, but how they are carried out depends on him. He will assume control of your cities, states, and nations. He is going to move in and take over your churches, schools, universities, and corporations....The fate of humanity is in his hands.*

Our fate is in very good shape. I am going to go give my children a hug now that I have written these last pages and tell them that I love them. I hope you will do the same with yours.

Appendix:
Resources for More Information

PARENTING IS CHALLENGING, and I expect that you have many questions that I did not address. I also know that there are times when we need more information about a particular topic than a general book can address. This appendix includes organizations, Web sites, and hotlines that you may find useful. We are lucky to be living at a time when we have access to a vast array of information on the Internet.

I have compiled this list of organizations to go with the chapters in this book. I understand that this list is not exhaustive, and I would welcome hearing from you about which sites have been most helpful. Please know that Web site addresses change quickly; this list is current as of this writing.

I also want to repeat something I said in the introduction: if you or your child is facing physical or mental health or safety issues, please contact your physician or mental health provider. No book or Web site can take the place of one-on-one help from a qualified professional.

GENERAL CHILD & ADOLESCENT HEALTH

American Academy of Pediatrics
141 Northwest Point Blvd.
Elk Grove Village, IL 60007
847-434-4000
www.aap.org

Includes parenting information on a range of health topics such as asthma, obesity, immunizations, and safety.

Dr. Spock
www.drspock.com

Provides information for parents of children of every age, including topics such as behavior and development, nutrition, health, and school issues.

Search Institute
The Banks Building
615 First Ave. NE, Suite 125
Minneapolis, MN 55413
800-888-7828
www.search-institute.org

Provides resources for parents on raising healthy kids, in the form of downloads or publications for purchase from its online store.

Society for Adolescent Medicine
1916 Copper Oaks Circle
Blue Springs, MO 64015
816-224-8010
www.adolescenthealth.org

Includes parenting information focusing on adolescents, including finding an adolescent health professional and preparing for the college years.

U.S. Department of Health and Human Services
200 Independence Ave. SW
Washington, DC 20201
877-696-6775

Healthfinder
www.healthfinder.gov/justforyou/justforyou.asp?KeyWordID=183&branch=1

A special section of the U.S. Department of Health and Human Services focusing on keeping parents and children healthy in mind, body, and spirit.

U.S. Centers for Disease Control and Prevention
1600 Clifton Rd.
Atlanta, GA 30333
Public Inquiries: 800-311-3435
www.cdc.gov/doc.do/id/0900f3ec802270e4

This section of the Centers for Disease Control Web site contains links to a variety of health topics dealing with infants and children, such as airbags, dog bites, head lice, and child abuse.

CHILDHOOD OBESITY

Obesity Society
1250 24th St. NW, Suite 300
Washington, DC 20037
202-776-7711
www.obesity.org

This organization gives background on childhood obesity, helps you to identify obesity in your child, cites health risks associated with obesity, and gives prevention advice.

Weight-control Information Network (WIN)
1 WIN Way
Bethesda, MD 20892
877-946-4627
E-mail: win@info.niddk.nih.gov
http://win.niddk.nih.gov/publications/child.htm

The Weight-control Information Network has a useful online publication that answers frequently asked questions about how to help children maintain a healthy weight and what to do if your child is overweight.

EATING DISORDERS

National Eating Disorders Association
603 Stewart St., Suite 803
Seattle, WA 98101
800-931-2237
www.nationaleatingdisorders.org

The National Eating Disorders Association has a wide variety of information on eating disorders, including a Parent and Family Network that has information for parents and families about treatment, resources, and advocacy.

Academy for Eating Disorders
60 Revere Dr., Suite 500
Northbrook, IL 60062
847-498-4274
www.aedweb.org

A professional organization whose goal is to promote research, treatment, and prevention of eating disorders. It provides information on diagnoses, treatment, and consequences of eating disorders.

Anorexia Nervosa and Related Eating Disorders, Inc. (ANRED)
www.anred.com

ANRED has merged with the National Eating Disorders Association but still keeps its Web site up-to-date with a wealth of information.

MENTAL HEALTH

American Academy of Child and Adolescent Psychiatry
www.aacap.org

Mental Health America (formerly National Mental Health Association)
2000 N. Beauregard St., 6th Floor
Alexandria, VA 22311
703-684-7722

Toll free: 800-969-6642
Fax: 703-684-5968
www.mentalhealthamerica.net

Contains information for parents on how to help their children cope with loss and information on prevention of mental and emotional disabilities, in addition to general information on children's mental health problems.

Federation of Families for Children's Mental Health (FFCMH)
9605 Medical Center Dr., Suite 280
Rockville, MD 20850
240-403-1901
www.ffcmh.org

Provides parents with tips and information, as well as publications and services for families of children with emotional, behavioral, and mental health issues.

National Alliance on Mental Illness (NAMI)
2107 Wilson Blvd., Suite 300
Arlington, VA 22201-3042
Helpline: 800-950-NAMI
www.nami.org
E-mail: info@nami.org

NAMI gives families a portal to inform and educate themselves, as well as find support from state and local alliances. Also gives families and members of the public an outlet for advocacy about mental illness in society.

National Institutes of Mental Health
6001 Executive Blvd., Room 8184, MSC 9663
Bethesda, MD 20892
301-443-4513
www.nimh.gov

This U.S. government Web site on mental health and mental illnesses includes wonderful fact sheets and resources for more information.

ADHD

Children and Adults with Attention Deficit/Hyperactivity Disorder
(CHADD)
8181 Professional Pl., Suite 150
Landover, MD 20785
301-306-7070
National Resource Center Hotline: 800-233-4050
www.chadd.org

Provides resources and information on ADHD, including specific information for parents on how to deal with ADHD while your child is in school.
Also gives parents a way to access support on a more personal level with
local chapters, national conferences, and parent-to-parent training.

Attention Deficit Disorder Association (ADDA)
15000 Commerce Pkwy., Suite C
Mount Laurel, NJ 08054
856-439-9099
www.add.org

Valuable resource for parents to access general information about ADHD,
especially for parents of older children who are making the transition to
adulthood.

ALCOHOL

Mothers Against Drunk Driving (MADD)
MADD National Office
511 E. John Carpenter Frwy., Suite 700
Irving, TX 75062
800-GET-MADD
24-hour Victim Services: 877-MADD-HELP
www.madd.org

MADD's mission is to stop drunk driving, to support its victims, and to prevent underage drinking. Its Web site contains statistics, laws, and information for parents about their teens and drinking.

National Council on Alcoholism and Drug Dependence (NCADD)
244 East 58th St., 4th Floor
New York, NY 10022
212-269-7797
Fax: 212-269-7510
E-mail: national@ncadd.org
www.ncadd.org

NCADD provides facts and information for parents about how to talk to your child about drinking, and how to know if he or she is in trouble with alcohol.

National Institute on Alcohol Abuse and Alcoholism (NIAAA)
Leadership to Keep Children Alcohol-Free
7500 Old Georgetown Rd., Suite 900
Bethesda, MD 20814
www.niaaa.nih.gov

This organization looks to prevent underage drinking in children ages 9–15. They have information and statistics for parents about what you can do, prevention strategies, and warning signs.

DRUGS

Substance Abuse and Mental Health Services Administration (SAMHSA)
Keeping Youth Mentally Healthy and Drug Free Family Guide
1 Choke Cherry Rd.
Rockville, MD 20857
Crisis Hotline: 800-273-8255
www.family.samhsa.gov

A family guide for parents about how to talk with children, get involved, and monitor their activities.

The Partnership for a Drug-Free America
405 Lexington Ave., Suite 1601
New York, NY 10174
212-922-1560
www.drugfree.org

Provides parenting information on how to connect with your children and spot drug use, and what to do if your kids are using drugs.

National Institute on Drug Abuse
6001 Executive Blvd., Room 5213
Bethesda, MD 20892
www.nida.nih.gov

Includes drug information and facts parents need to know about specific drugs, and has statistics on trends in drugs.

Parents. The Anti-Drug.
800-729-6686
www.theantidrug.com

A Web site created specifically for parents that contains drug information, advice, and how to know if your teen is using drugs.

The National Center on Addiction and Substance Abuse (CASA)
633 Third Ave., 19th Floor
New York, NY 10017-6706
212-841-5200
www.casacolumbia.org

CASA at Columbia University provides up-to-date statistics and information on drugs and alcohol.

SEXUALITY

Advocates for Youth
2000 M St. NW, Suite 750
Washington, DC 20036
202-419-3420
www.advocatesforyouth.org/parents/index.htm

Advocates for Youth has a Sex Ed Center for parents that addresses issues such as talking about sexuality and contraception with teens.

SIECUS
130 West 42nd St., Suite 350
New York, NY 10036
212-819-9770
www.familiesaretalking.org

The Sexuality Information and Education Council of the United States has developed a separate Web site for parents on sexuality education in the home.

Planned Parenthood Federation of America
434 West 33rd St.
New York, NY 10001
212-541-7800
www.plannedparenthood.org

Official gateway to the online Planned Parenthood community, which provides sexual and reproductive health care education. Web site provides reproductive health and rights information, services, and resources.

CHILD ABUSE PREVENTION

National Center for Missing and Exploited Children
Charles B. Wang International Children's Building
699 Prince St.
Alexandria, VA 22314
703-274-3900
Hotline: 800-THE-LOST
www.missingkids.com

Resources for parents on prevention of abduction and exploitation of children, including information on how to keep children safe while on the Web, and assistance and information for parents whose children have been victimized.

Child Welfare Information Gateway
Children's Bureau/ACYF
1250 Maryland Ave. SW, 8th Floor
Washington, DC 20024

800-394-3366
ChildHelp Hotline: 800-422-4453
www.childwelfare.gov

This site provides information for parents to help protect children and strengthen families.

Prevent Child Abuse America
500 N. Michigan Ave., Suite 200
Chicago, IL 60611
312-663-8962
www.preventchildabuse.org

This Web site provides tips on the prevention of child abuse and allows parents to get in touch with their local chapters of the organization.

Stop It Now!
351 Pleasant St., Suite B-319
Northampton, MA 01060
413-587-3500
Helpline : 888-PREVENT
www.stopitnow.org

Stop It Now!'s Web site gives warning signs of sexual abuse in children, has an online resource guide, and allows access to publications on the prevention of sexual abuse in children.

Darkness to Light, Child Sexual Abuse Prevention
7 Radcliffe St., Suite 200
Charleston, SC 29403
Helpline: 866-FOR-LIGHT
www.darkness2light.org

Information for parents and adults about child sex abuse, where to get help, and ways to prevent it.

INTERNET SAFETY

There are a number of Web sites that include information on Internet safety for parents, children, and teenagers. Here are some that offer good information:

Webwisekids.org   Safeteens.com
Wiredsafety.org   Safekids.com
Blogsafety.org   Netsmartz.org
Getnetwise.org

SCHOOLS

PTA
541 N Fairbanks Court, Suite 1300
Chicago, IL 60611
312-670-6782
www.pta.org

The Parent Teacher Association has resources for parents that focus on student achievement, safety, media technology, and health and wellness.

National Education Association (NEA)
1201 16th Street NW
Washington, DC 20036
202-833-4000
www.nea.org

Advises parents on how to get involved in their children's education.

American Library Association (ALA)
50 East Huron St.
Chicago, IL 60611
800-545-2433
www.ala.org

A great resource to educate and inform parents about a variety of topics.

Notes

Page

INTRODUCTION. IS PARENTING HARDER TODAY?

1   "8 in 10 parents": Public Agenda, "A Lot Easier Said Than Done: Parents Talk About Raising Children in Today's America," www.publicagenda.org/specials/parents/parents4.htm.

CHAPTER 1. NEW CHALLENGES AND NEW SOLUTIONS

13   Jodi Picoult in *It's a Boy: Women Writers on Raising Sons*, ed. Andrea Buchanan (Emeryville, CA: Seal Press, 2005).

16   Public Agenda survey: "Kids These Days '99: What Americans Really Think About the Next Generation," March 26, 2006, www.publicagenda. org/specials/kids/kids.htm.

CHAPTER 2. AFFIRMING PARENTS

23   Quote from Dr. Baumrind: Diana Baumrind, "Effects of Authoritative Parental Control on Child Behavior," *Child Development* 37, No. 4 (December 1966): 887–907.

CHAPTER 3. THEIR BODIES, THEIR SELVES: RAISING PHYSICALLY HEALTHY CHILDREN

46   Dr. Ouellette quote in Anita Manning, "Measles Remains a Threat Despite 'Eradication,'" *USA Today*, July 2006.

Page

46 Study of girls' early breast development: Marcia Herman-Giddens, "Recent Data on Pubertal Milestones," *International Journal of Andrology* 29, No. 1 (2006): 241–46.

48 "There are no published data...": Hans Wijbrand Hoek and Daphne van Hoeken, "Review of the Prevalence and Incidence of Eating Disorders," *International Journal of Eating Disorders* 34, No. 4 (January 26, 2003): 383–96.

51 "from 41.8 percent to 45.6 percent": All comparisons from 1991 on in this chapter are from the U.S. Centers for Disease Control and Prevention, National Youth Risk Behavior Survey (www.cdc.gov).

54 Information and statistics on anorexia are from National Association of Anorexia Nervosa and Associated Disorders, "Facts About Eating Disorders," www.anad.org/site/anadweb/content.php?type=1&id= 6982.

55 *Newsweek* article: Peg Tyre, "Fighting Anorexia: No One to Blame," *Newsweek* (December 5, 2005), www.msnbc.msn.com/id/10219756/ site/newsweek.

CHAPTER 4. THE MYTH OF THE OVERSCHEDULED, OVERSTRESSED GENERATION

64 "A 2000 poll of 84,000 young people": from the Search Institute's "Developmental Assets" reports.

64 Dr. Hofferth: Unless otherwise noted, the data in this chapter about children's use of time are from Sandra Hofferth's studies of 1981, 1997, and 2003: Sandra L. Hofferth and Sally Curtin, "Changes in Children's Time, 1997 to 2002/3: An Update," Unpublished ms. January 2006; Sandra Hofferth and John F. Sandberg, "Changes in American Children's Time, 1981–1997," *Children at the Millennium: Where Have We Come From, Where Are We Going?* (New York: Elsevier Science, 2001), pp. 193–229.

65 Data about adults' use of time are from the Bureau of Labor Statistics' American Time Use Survey from 2005.

72 Johns Hopkins University study: Karen Ablard and Wayne Parker, "Parents' Achievement Goals and Perfectionism in Their Academically Talented Children," *Journal of Youth and Adolescence* 26 (1997): 651–67.

Page

CHAPTER 5. KNOWING THEIR MINDS: RAISING
EMOTIONALLY HEALTHY CHILDREN

80 ADHD became the preferred name in the psychiatric profession's standard list, *The Diagnostic and Statistical Manual of Mental Disorders*, in 1987.

80 Dr. Paul Steinberg: Paul Steinberg, "Attention Surplus? Re-examining a Disorder," *New York Times*, March 7, 2006, p. F6.

80 *American Journal of Public Health* article cited in Kim Painter, "Send Your Kids Outside—Now," *USA Today*, March 20, 2006, p. 4D.

82 Unless otherwise noted, all childhood mental health statistics are from U.S. Department of Health and Human Services 1999 and U.S. Centers for Disease Control Youth Risk Behavior Surveys 1991–2005 (www.cdc.gov).

82 Suicide statistics from Centers for Disease Control and Prevention, "Deaths, Percent of Total Deaths, and Death Rates for the 15 Leading Causes of Death in 10-Year Age Groups by Race and Sex" (2003), www.cdc.gov/nchs/data/dvs/lcwk2_2003.pdf.

83 "In one study, parents sought help..." Suniya S. Luthar and Bronwyn E. Becker, "Privileged But Pressured? A Study of Affluent Youth," *Child Development* 73, No. 5 (2002): 1593–1610.

CHAPTER 6. JUST SAY KNOW: RAISING SEXUALLY
HEALTHY CHILDREN

91 "high-quality national studies": For comprehensive reviews of oral sex and teenagers, see Nora Gelperin, "Oral Sex and Young Adolescents," *Educator's Update* 9, No. 1 (August 2004); and Lisa Remez, "Oral Sex Among Adolescents: Is It Sex or Is It Abstinence?" *Family Planning Perspectives* 32, No. 6 (November/December 2000).

95 "Research studies show...": see Michael D. Resnick et al., "Protecting Adolescents from Harm: Findings from the National Longitudinal Study on Adolescents," *Journal of the American Medical Association* 278 (September 10, 1997).

96 "Good News" section: All trend data for sexual behaviors and contraceptive use are from the U.S. Centers for Disease Control, National Youth Risk Behavior Surveys 1991–2005 (www.cdc.gov).

97 "Guttmacher Institute...estimates that 85 percent": Guttmacher Institute, "Teenagers in the United States: Sexual Activity,

Page

Contraceptive Use, and Childbearing" (2002), www.cdc.gov/nchs/
data/series/sr_23/sr23_024.pdf.

97 "Rates of most sexually transmitted diseases...": Guttmacher
Institute, "Sexually Transmitted Diseases Among American Youth,"
www.guttmacher.org/pubs/journals/3600604.html, and American
Social Health Association, "State of the Nation 2005: Challenges
Facing STD Prevention in Youth," 2005.

100 Oral sex statistics: Ed Laumann et al., *The Social Organization of
Sexuality: Sexual Practices in the United States* (Chicago: University of
Chicago Press, 1994).

101 *Journal of the American Medical Association*: Stephanie A. Sanders and
June Reinish, "Would You Say You 'Had Sex' If?," *Journal of the
American Medical Association* 281 (1999): 275–77.

102 study of ninth graders from California: Bonnie Halpern-Fisher et. al.,
"Oral versus Vaginal Sex Among Adolescents: Perceptions, Attitudes,
and Behaviors," *Pediatrics* 115, No. 4 (April 2005): 845–51.

103 Statistics on sexual orientation from Timothy Palmer and Debra
Haffner, *A Time to Seek* (CT: Religious Institute, 2007).

103 "study of religious teens" cited in Steve Clapp, Kristen L. Helbert, and
Angela Zizak, *Faith Matters: Teenagers, Religion, and Sexuality* (Fort
Wayne, IN: Lifequest, 2003).

104 "at least 1 in 6 women": Boston Women's Health Book Collective,
Our Bodies, Ourselves (2005).

106 "A study of more than twelve thousand teenagers...": Michael D.
Resnick et al., "Protecting Adolescents from Harm: Findings from the
National Longitudinal Study on Adolescents." *Journal of the American
Medical Association* 278 (September 10, 1997).

106 "studies have found that the more moms...": See, e.g., Laurie L.
Meschke, Suzanne Bartholomae, and Shannon R. Sentall,
"Adolescent Sexuality and Parent-Adolescent Processes: Promoting
Healthy Teen Choices," *Family Relations* 49, No. 2 (2000): 143–54.

106 Paragraph beginning "On the other hand...": Douglas Kirby, B. Laris,
and Lori Rolleri, "The Impact of Sex and HIV Education Programs in
Schools and Communities" (NC: Family Health International, 2006).

Page

CHAPTER 7. SOBERING NEWS: ALCOHOL, DRUGS, AND
RAISING RESPONSIBLE CHILDREN

113   Trend data from 1991 to 2005 on alcohol and drugs are from the U.S. Centers for Disease Control and Prevention, National Youth Risk Behavior Surveys (www.cdc.gov); comparisons with 1975 are from the National Institute on Drug Abuse, Monitoring the Future Survey 2004.

114   "lowest rates of drinking in thirty-eight years": "The American Freshman: National Norms for 2006," posted at http://gseis. ucla.edu/heri/norms06.php.

115   University of Mississippi test: University of Mississippi Marijuana Potency Monitoring Project, Report 95, January 9, 2007.

118   Dr. Suniya Luthar: Suniya S. Luthar and Karen D'Avanzo, "Contextual Factors in Substance Use: A Study of Suburban and Inner-City Adolescents," *Development and Psychopathology* 11 (1999): 845–67.

121   National Survey of Drug Use and Health: http://oas.samhsa. gov/2K6/getpain/getpain.cfm.

122   "studies in several states found…": Donald Lynman et al., "Project DARE: No Effects at 10-Year Follow-up," *Journal of Consulting and Clinical Psychology* 67 (1999): 590–93.

124   "Research indicates that parents can help delay": See, e.g., Michael D. Resnick et al., "Protecting Adolescents from Harm: Findings from the National Longitudinal Study on Adolescents," *Journal of the American Medical Association* 278 (September 10, 1997).

126   "In studies, teenagers who do not anticipate…": Suniya S. Luthar and Karen D'Avanzo, "Contextual Factors in Substance Use: A Study of Suburban and Inner-City Adolescents," *Development and Psychopathology* 11 (1999): 845–67.

127   alcohol use in rats: Linda Patia Spear, "The Adolescent Brain and the College Drinker," *Journal of Studies on Alcohol* (2002): 71–81.

CHAPTER 8. THE TRUTH ABOUT ABDUCTIONS AND
SEXUAL ABUSE

134   Jonathan Fast, personal communication.

136   Department of Justice: All data on missing children in this chapter are from David Finkelhor, Heather Hammer, and Andrea J. Sedlak,

Page

"Nonfamily Abducted Children: National Estimates and Characteristics," *National Incidence Studies of Missing, Abducted, Runaway, and Thrownaway Children* (October 2002); and Andrea J. Sedlak, David Finkelhor, Heather Hammer, and Dana J. Schultz, "National Estimates of Missing Children: An Overview," *National Incidence Studies of Missing, Abducted, Runaway, and Thrownaway Children* (October 2002).

139   "Facing the Realities of Sexual Abuse": Unless stated otherwise, sources for statistics are from Federal Center for Sex Offender Management; National Center for Juvenile Justice; and Bureau of Justice Statistics. For a comprehensive review of child sexual abuse, see Debra Haffner, *A Time to Heal* (Life Quest Publications, 2005).

CHAPTER 9. COUCH POTATO, MOUSE POTATO: NAVIGATING THE NEW ELECTRONIC WORLD

147   The major sources for the data on media usage in this chapter are the Kaiser Family Foundation surveys and reports (www.kff.org) and Donald F. Roberts, Ulla G. Foehr, and Victoria Rideout, "Generation M: Media in the Lives of 8-18 Year-Olds," *Kaiser Family Foundation Study*, March 2005.

149   *Pediatrics* study: Tara Stevens and Miriam Moslow, "There Is No Meaningful Association Between Television Exposure and Symptoms of ADHD," *Pediatrics* 117 (2006): 665–72.

151   All data on online solicitations are from Powerpoint presentations at "Electronic Media and Youth Violence Expert Panel," Sept. 20–21, 2006, sponsored by the Division of Violence, U.S. Centers for Disease Control.

153   All data on teenagers socializing online synthesized from Kaiser Family Foundation, "Key Facts: Teens Online," No. 3293, Nov. 20, 2002; and U.S. Department of Commerce, "A Nation Online: Entering the Broadband Age," September 2004.

155   *New York Times* article: "Teenagers Misbehaving in New York Suburbs, Now for All the Internet World to Watch," February 13, 2007.

160   "38 percent of parents have never seen their teenagers' online pro-file": Edward C. Baig, "Where's Junior? The Phone Knows," *USA Today*, April 20, 2006, p. B3.

Page

CHAPTER 10. RAISING A MENSCH: THE IMPORTANCE OF
ETHICS AND SPIRITUALITY IN YOUR CHILD'S WORLD

168   14 percent: Eugene C. Roehlkepartain, Pamela Ebstyne King, Linda
Wagener, and Peter L. Benson, *The Handbook of Spiritual Development
in Childhood and Adolescence* (Thousand Oaks, CA: Sage Publications,
2006).

169   Dr. James Fowler quoted in Roehlkepartain et al., *Handbook of
Spiritual Development.*

181   "Religious teens have half the rate of sexual intercourse...": Steve
Clapp, Kristen L. Helbert, and Angela Zizak, *Faith Matters: Teenagers,
Religion, and Sexuality* (Fort Wayne, IN: Lifequest, 2003).

182   Higher Education Research Institute statistics: Beth Walton,
"Volunteer Rates Hit Record Numbers," *USA Today*, July 6, 2006,
www.usatoday.com/news/ation/2006-07-06-volunteers_x.htm.

References

Ablard, Karen, and Wayne Parker. "Parents' Achievement Goals and Perfectionism in Their Academically Talented Children." *Journal of Youth and Adolescence* 26 (1997): 651–67.

Adams, Jane Lubchansky. "The Kids Aren't All Right." *Smith Alumni Quarterly,* http://saqonline.smith.edu/article.epl?issue_id=4&article_id=141.

American Academy of Pediatrics, Committee on Substance Abuse. "Marijuana: A Continuing Concern for Pediatrics." *Pediatrics* 104, no. 4 (October 1999).

American Social Health Association. "State of the Nation 2005: Challenges Facing STD Prevention in Youth," 2005.

Apter, Terri. *The Myth of Maturity: What Teenagers Need from Parents to Become Adults.* New York: W. W. Norton, 2002.

Aquilino, William S., and Andrew J. Supple. "Long-Term Effects of Parenting Practices During Adolescence on Well-Being Outcomes in Young Adulthood." *Journal of Family Issues* 22, no. 3 (April 2001): 289–308.

Ary, Dennis V., Terry E. Duncan, Anthony Biglan, Carol W. Metzler, John W. Noell, and Keith Smolkowski. "Development of Adolescent Problem Behavior." *Journal of Abnormal Child Psychology* 27, no. 2 (1999): 141–50.

Ary, Dennis V., Terry E. Duncan, Susan C. Duncan, and Hyman Hops. "Adolescent Problem Behavior: The Influence of Parents and Peers." *Behaviour Research and Therapy* 37 (1999): 217–30.

Baig, Edward C. "Where's Junior? The Phone Knows." *USA Today*, April 20, 2006, p. B3.

Barber, Brian K. "Parental Psychological Control: Revisiting a Neglected Construct," *Child Development* 67 (1996): 3296–3319.

Baumrind, Diana. "The Influence of Parenting Style on Adolescent Competence and Substance Use." *Journal of Early Adolescence* 11, no. 1 (1991): 56–95.

———. "Effects of Authoritative Parental Control on Child Behavior." *Child Development* 37, no. 4 (December 1966): 887–907.

Belkin, Lisa. "A Leader at Work, Sometimes Lost at Home." *New York Times*, March 26, 2006.

Borowsky, Iris Wagman, Marjorie Ireland, and Michael D. Resnick. "Adolescent Suicide Attempts: Risks and Protectors." *Pediatrics* 107, no. 3 (March 2001).

Brucker, H., and P. S. Bearman. "After the Promise: The STD Consequences of Adolescent Virginity Pledges." *Journal of Adolescent Health* 36 (2005): 271–78.

Buchanan, Andrea, ed. *It's a Boy: Women Writers on Raising Sons* (Emeryville, CA: Seal Press, 2005).

Bureau of Justice Statistics, http://www.ojp.usdooj.gov/bjs/abstract/rsorp94.htm.

Center for the Prevention of Sexual and Domestic Violence. "Fact Sheet," www.cpsdv.org/Child-Abuse/index.htm.

Centers for Disease Control and Prevention. "Youth Online: Comprehensive Results." September 2004.

———. Morbidity Mortality Weekly Report 53 (2004) (SS-2): 1–29.

———. "Deaths, Percent of Total Deaths, and Death Rates for the 15 Leading Causes of Death in 10-Year Age Groups by Race and Sex" (2003), http://www.cdc.gov/nchs/data/dvs/lcwk2_2003.pdf.

———. "Trends in the Prevalence of Sexual Behaviors." *National Youth Risk Behavior Survey: 1991–2005* (2005).

———. "Overweight Among U.S. Children and Adolescents." *National Health and Nutrition Examination Survey* (1994), http://www.cdc.gov/nchs/data/nhanes/databriefs/overwght.pdf.

Clapp, Steve, Kristen L. Helbert, and Angela Zizak. *Faith Matters: Teenagers, Religion, and Sexuality*. Fort Wayne, IN: Lifequest, 2003.

Clements, Dennis. "Restless Kids with Restless Minds." *Duke Health* (Sept. 16, 2006), http://www.dukehealth.org/dr_clements/adhd?print-friendly=1.

Faden, Vivian B. "Trends in Initiation of Alcohol Use in the United States: 1975 to 2003." *Alcoholism: Clinical and Experimental Research* 30, no. 6 (June 2006).

Federal Center for Sex Offender Management. "Recidivism of Sex Offenders," www.csom.org/pubs/recidsexof.html.

Finkelhor, David, Heather Hammer, and Andrea J. Sedlak. "Nonfamily Abducted Children: National Estimates and Characteristics." *National Incidence Studies of Missing, Abducted, Runaway, and Thrownaway Children* (October 2002).

Fisher, Helen. *Why We Love: The Nature and Chemistry of Romantic Love*. New York: Holt, 2004.

Fombonne, Eric, and Suniti Chakrabarti. "No Evidence for a New Variant of Measles-Mumps-Rubella-Induced Autism." *Pediatrics* 108, no. 58 (2001).

Garbarino, James, and Claire Bedard. *Parents Under Siege: Why You Are the Solution, Not the Problem, in Your Child's Life*. New York: Free Press, 2002.

Gelperin, Nora. "Oral Sex and Young Adolescents," *Educator's Update* 9, no. 1 (August 2004).

Gibbs, Nancy, and Nathan Thornburgh. "Who Needs Harvard?" *Time* 168, no. 8, August 21, 2006.

Gross, Jane. "Checklist for Camp: Bug Spray. Sunscreen. Pills." *The New York Times*, July 16, 2006, p. A1.

Guttmacher Institute. "Sexually Transmitted Diseases Among American Youth," http://www.guttmacher.org/pubs/journals/3600604.html.

———. "Teenagers in the United States: Sexual Activity, Contraceptive Use, and Childbearing" (2002), http://www.cdc.gov/nchs/data/series/sr _23/sr23_024.pdf.

Haffner, Debra. *A Time to Heal*. Life Quest Publications, 2005.

Haffner, Debra W., and Larry L. Greenfield. "Youth Development and Faith-Based Institutions." *Religious Institute Study Notes* (2003).

Halpern-Fisher, Bonnie, et. al. "Oral versus Vaginal Sex Among Adolescents: Perceptions, Attitudes, and Behaviors." *Pediatrics* 115, no. 4 (April 2005): 845–51.

Haynes, Charles C. "A Moral Battleground, a Civil Discourse." *USA Today,* March 20, 2006, p. 15A.

HealthyPlace.com. "When Very Young Kids Have Eating Disorders," http://www.healthyplace.com/Communities/Eating_Disorders/children_1.asp.

Hempel, Jessi. "Family Matters: Your Child's Bodyguard in the Sky." *Time,* May 8, 2006, p. 14.

Herman-Giddens, Marcia. "Recent Data on Pubertal Milestones." *International Journal of Andrology* 29, no. 1 (2006): 241–46.

Hoek, Hans Wijbrand, and Daphne van Hoeken. "Review of the Prevalence and Incidence of Eating Disorders." *International Journal of Eating Disorders* 34, no. 4 (January 26, 2003): 383–96.

Hofferth, Sandra L., and Sally Curtin. "Changes in Children's Time, 1997 to 2002/3: An Update." Unpublished ms. January 2006.

Hofferth, Sandra, and John F. Sandberg. "Changes in American Children's Time, 1981–1997." *Children at the Millennium: Where Have We Come From, Where Are We Going?* New York: Elsevier Science, 2001, pp. 193–229.

———. "How American Children Spend Their Time." *Journal of Marriage and Family* 63 (May 2001): 295–308.

Hulbert, Ann. *Raising America: Experts, Parents, and a Century of Advice About Children.* New York: Knopf, 2003.

Insurance Institute for Highway Safety. "Fatality Facts 2004: Teenagers," Highway Loss Data Institute (2004), http://www.iihs.org/research/fatality_facts/teenagers.html#sec1.

Jayson, Sharon. "Report: Teenagers Often Shun Condoms." *USA Today,* Aug. 3, 2006, p. 6D.

Johnson, D. Gale. "Population, Food, and Knowledge." *American Economic Review* 90, no. 1 (March 2000): 11.

Johnson, Steven. "What's Next Forum," *Time,* March 20, 2006.

Kaiser Family Foundation. "Sex on TV," no. 7398, Nov. 9, 2005.

———. "Sex Smarts Survey: Virginity and the First Time," no. 3368 (2003).

————. "Key Facts: Teens Online," no. 3293, Nov. 20, 2002.

Kindlon, Dan. *Too Much of a Good Thing: Raising Children of Character in an Indulgent Age.* New York: Miramax Books, 2001.

Kirby, Douglas, B. Laris, and Lori Rolleri. "The Impact of Sex and HIV Education Programs in Schools and Communities." NC: Family Health International, 2006.

Kirn, Walter, and Wendy Cole. "What Ever Happened to Play?" *Time,* April 22, 2001.

Lamborn, Susie D., Nina S. Mounts, Laurence Steinberg, and Sanford M. Dornbusch. "Patterns of Competence and Adjustment Among Adolescents from Authoritative, Authoritarian, Indulgent, and Neglectful Families." *Child Development* 62 (1991): 1049–65.

Laumann, Ed, et al. *The Social Organization of Sexuality: Sexual Practices in the United States.* Chicago: University of Chicago Press, 1994.

Lenhart, Amanda, Mary Madden, and Paul Hitlin. "Teens and Technology: Youth Are Leading the Transition to a Fully Wired and Mobile Nation," *Pew Internet & American Life Project,* July 27, 2005.

Levine, Michael. "10 Things Parents Can Do to Help Prevent Eating Disorders," www.nationaleatingdisorders.org.

Linn, Susan. "How Can I Raise a Moral Child?" February 25, 2006, http://www.familyeducation.com/article/print/0,1303,20-13164,00.html?obj.gra.

Luthar, Suniya S., and Bronwyn E. Becker. "Privileged but Pressured? A Study of Affluent Youth." *Child Development* 73, no. 5 (2002): 1593–1610.

Luthar, Suniya S., and Karen D'Avanzo. "Contextual Factors in Substance Use: A Study of Suburban and Inner-City Adolescents." *Development and Psychopathology* 11 (1999): 845–67.

Lynman, Donald, et al. "Project DARE: No Effects at 10-Year Follow-up." *Journal of Consulting and Clinical Psychology* 67 (1999): 590–93.

Madsen, Kreesten Meldgaard, et al. "A Population-Based Study of Measles, Mumps, and Rubella Vaccination and Autism." *New England Journal of Medicine* 347, no. 19 (Nov. 7, 2002).

Males, Mike. "Gutless About Gut Issues." *Youth Today* (September 2003).

Manning, Anita. "Measles Remains a Threat Despite 'Eradication.'" *USA Today,* July 2006.

Mausner, Judith, and Anita Bahn. *Epidemiology: An Introductory Text.* Philadelphia: W. B. Saunders, 1974.

Meschke, Laurie L., Suzanne Bartholomae, and Shannon R. Sentall. "Adolescent Sexuality and Parent-Adolescent Processes: Promoting Healthy Teen Choices." *Family Relations* 49, no. 2 (2000): 143–54.

National Association of Anorexia Nervosa and Associated Disorders. "Facts About Eating Disorders," http://www.anad.org/site/anadweb/content.php?type=1&id=6982.

National Institute on Drug Abuse. "National Survey Results on Drug Use, 1975–2004." *Monitoring the Future Survey* (2004): 283–96.

New York Times. "Record Highs and Lows: Good Behavior," April 23, 2006, p. 7.

Painter, Kim. "Send Your Kids Outside—Now." *USA Today,* March 20, 2006, p. 4D.

Palmer, Timothy, and Debra Haffner. *A Time to Seek.* CT: Religious Institute, 2007.

Partsch, C-J, and W. G. Sippell. "Pathogenesis and Epidemiology of Precocious Puberty: Effects of Exogenous Oestrogens." *Human Reproduction Update* 7, no. 3 (2001): 292–302.

Pear, Robert. "Married and Single Parents Spending More Time with Children, Study Finds." *New York Times,* Oct. 17, 2006, p. A12.

Pittman, Laura D., and P. Lindsay Chase-Lansdale. "African American Adolescent Girls in Impoverished Communities: Parenting Style and Adolescent Outcomes." *Journal of Research on Adolescence* 11, no. 2 (2001): 199–224.

Pollard, Peter. "Many Paths to Prevention." *Stop It Now! News* 14, no. 1 (2006): 2.

Public Agenda. "Kids These Days '99: What Americans Really Think About the Next Generation," March 26, 2006, www.publicagenda. org/specials/kids/kids.htm.

———. "A Lot Easier Said Than Done: Parents Talk About Raising Children in Today's America," www.publicagenda.org/specials/parents/parents4.htm.

———. "Americans Deeply Troubled About Nation's Youth; Even Young Children Described by Majority in Negative Terms," 1997, http://www.publicagenda.org/press/press_release_detail.cfm?list=7.

Remez, Lisa. "Oral Sex Among Adolescents: Is It Sex or Is It Abstinence?" *Family Planning Perspectives* 32, no. 6 (November/December 2000).

Renfrew Center Foundation for Eating Disorders. "How to Help a Friend or Family Member," http://www.renfrewcenter.com/for-family-friends/index.asp#prevention.

Resnick, Michael D., Marjorie Ireland, and Iris Borowsky. "Youth Violence Perpetration: What Protects? What Predicts? Findings from the National Longitudinal Study of Adolescent Health." *Journal of Adolescent Health.* New York: Society for Adolescent Medicine, 2004.

Resnick, Michael D., and Peggy Mann Rinehart. "Influencing Behavior: The Power of Protective Factors in Reducing Youth Violence," University of Minnesota, 2004.

Resnick, Michael D., et al. "Protecting Adolescents from Harm: Findings from the National Longitudinal Study on Adolescents." *Journal of the American Medical Association* 278 (September 10, 1997).

Rhee, Kyung E., et al. "Parenting Styles and Overweight Status in First Grade," October 31, 2005, www.pediatrics.org/cgi/doi/10.1542.

Roberts, Donald F., Ulla G. Foehr, and Victoria Rideout. "Generation M: Media in the Lives of 8–18 Year-Olds." *Kaiser Family Foundation Study,* March 2005.

Roehlkepartain, Eugene C., Pamela Ebstyne King, Linda Wagener, and Peter L. Benson. *The Handbook of Spiritual Development in Childhood and Adolescence.* Thousand Oaks, CA: Sage Publications, 2006.

Safe Kids USA. "Accidental Injury Related Death for Children 14 and Under" (2004), http://www.usa.safekids.org/tier3_cd_2c.cfm?content_item_id=19010&folder_id=540.

Sanders, Matthew R. "Triple P-Positive Parenting Program: Towards an Empirically Validated Multilevel Parenting and Family Support Strategy for the Prevention of Behavior and Emotional Problems in Children." *Clinical Child and Family Psychology Review* 2, no. 2 (1999).

Sanders, Stephanie A., and June Reinish. "Would You Say You 'Had Sex' If?" *Journal of the American Medical Association* 281 (1999): 275–77.

Santelli, John, et al. "Explaining Recent Declines in Adolescent Pregnancy." *American Journal of Public Health* 97 (2007): 150–56.

Sedlak, Andrea J., David Finkelhor, Heather Hammer, and Dana J. Schultz. "National Estimates of Missing Children: An Overview." *National Incidence Studies of Missing, Abducted, Runaway, and Thrownaway Children,* October 2002.

Shaw, Benjamin A., Neal Krause, Linda M. Chatters, Cathleen M. Connell, and Berit Ingersoll-Dayton. "Emotional Support from Parents Early in Life, Aging, and Health." *Psychology and Aging* 19, no. 1 (2004): 4–12.

Spear, Linda Patia. "The Adolescent Brain and the College Drinker." *Journal of Studies on Alcohol* (2002): 71–81.

Shoda, Yuichi, Walter Mischel, and Philip K. Peake. "Predicting Adolescent Cognitive and Self-Regulatory Competencies from Preschool Delay of Gratification: Identifying Diagnostic Conditions." *Developmental Psychology* 26, no. 6 (1990): 978–86.

Snyder, Howard J. "Sexual Assault of Young Children as Reported to Law Enforcement: Victim, Incident, and Offender Characteristics." Washington, DC: National Center for Juvenile Justice (2000).

Sprinkle, Robert Hunt. "The Missing Politics and Unsettled Science of the Trend Toward Earlier Puberty," *Politics and the Life Sciences* 20, no. 1 (March 2001): 43–66.

Steinberg, Paul. "Attention Surplus? Re-examining a Disorder." *New York Times*, March 7, 2006, p. F6.

Stevens, Tara, and Miriam Moslow. "There Is No Meaningful Association Between Television Exposure and Symptoms of ADHD." *Pediatrics* 117 (2006): 665–72.

Trickey, Helyn. "Eating Disorders Exact Toll on Adults, Too." *CNN.com*, March 24, 2006.

Tyre, Peg. "Fighting Anorexia: No One to Blame." *Newsweek* (December 5, 2005), http://www.msnbc.msn.com/id/10219756/site/newsweek.

University of Washington. "Teaching Adults More Effective Parenting Skills Is Best Tool for Treating Children with Serious Conduct Problems," http://www.uwnews.org/public/print2.asp.

U.S. Department of Commerce. "A Nation Online: Entering the Broadband Age," September 2004.

U.S. Department of Health and Human Services. *Mental Health: A Report of the Surgeon General* (1999): 150–63.

Wallis, Claudia. "Are Kids Too Wired for Their Own Good?" *Time*, March 27, 2006, p. 48.

Walton, Beth. "Volunteer Rates Hit Record Numbers." *USA Today*, July 6, 2006, http://www.usatoday.com/news/ation/2006-07-06-volunteers_x.htm.

Yust, Karen Marie, Aoestre N. Johnson, Sandy Eisenberg Sasso, and Eugene C. Roehlkepartain. *Nurturing Child and Adolescent Spirituality: Perspectives from the World's Religious Traditions*. Lanham, MD: Rowman & Littlefield, 2006.

Index

About the Author

Debra W. Haffner, M.Div., M.P.H, has been a parenting educator for more than twenty-five years and has provided presentations to thousands of parent and professional groups, including the National School Boards Association, the U.S. Centers for Disease Control and Prevention, the American Medical Association, the American Psychological Association, and public and private schools throughout the U.S. She speaks regularly about parenting issues, and is a contributor to *The Huffington Post*, has written for WebMD, iVillage, and DrSpock.com, and has been featured on *Oprah, The View, Today*, and in *Time, Newsweek, USA Today*, and *U.S. News & World Report*.

She is the author of six books, including *From Diapers to Dating: A Parent's Guide to Raising Sexually Healthy Children, Beyond the Big Talk: A Parent's Guide to Raising Sexually Healthy Teens*, and *What Every 21st-Century Parent Needs to Know: Facing Today's Challenges with Wisdom and Heart*.

The recipient of the Distinguished Alumni Award from the Department of Epidemiology and Public Health, Yale University School of Medicine, in 2000, Haffner holds a master's in public health from the Yale University School of Medicine and a master of divinity from Union Theological Seminary. Currently the director of the Religious Institute, she is also an ordained minister with the Unitarian Church in Westport, Connecticut. She previously served for twelve years as president and CEO of SIECUS, the Sexuality Information and Education Council of the United States.

She and her husband are the parents of two children, an adult daughter and a teenage son.

117329